Broadcast Writing

ELECTRONIC MEDIA GUIDES

Broadcast Writing

Dramas, Comedies, and Documentaries

Ken Dancyger

York University, Toronto, Canada

Focal Press
Boston   London

Focal Press is an imprint of Butterworth–Heinemann.

Recognizing the importance of preserving what has been written, it is the policy of Butterworth–Heinemann to have the books it publishes printed on acid-free paper, and we exert our best efforts to that end.

Library of Congress Cataloging-in-Publication Data
Dancyger, Ken.
    Broadcast writing: dramas, comedies, and documentaries / by Ken Dancyger.
          p.   cm. —(Electronic media guide)
    Includes bibliographical references.
    ISBN 0-240-80054-0 (paperback)
    1. Broadcasting—Authorship.   I. Title. II. Series.
    PN1992.7.D36   1991
    808'.066791—dc20   90-40739
                                           CIP

British Library Cataloguing in Publication Data
Dancyger, Ken
    Broadcast writing: dramas, comedies, and documentaries—(Electronic media guide)
    1. Scripts. Composition
    I. Title II. Series
    808.066

    ISBN 0-240-80054-0

Butterworth–Heinemann
80 Montvale Avenue
Stoneham, MA 02180

10 9 8 7 6 5 4 3 2 1 **166568**

Printed in the United States of America

For my parents,
Manya and Jack Dancyger
and
to the memory of my favorite in-laws,
Malka and Mendel Flint

Contents

Acknowledgments

Broadcast Writing is a book suggested to me by Karen Speerstra, Senior Editor at Focal Press. Karen has expressed considerable confidence in me and I owe her not only my deep gratitude for that confidence but also a public acknowledgment that were it not for her, I wouldn't have written this book.

Here in Toronto, there are several people I want to thank. I'd like to thank Michael Stokes for typing the manuscript. I'd like to thank Teresa Gordon for the photocopying. Critical to the preparation of the manuscript, it's a pleasure to be able to publicly thank George Robinson who has, above and beyond the call of duty, assisted me on numerous projects. On *Broadcast Writing*, he prepared the final manuscript, with all the organizational and logistical dimensions that role implies.

Finally, I would like to thank my wife Ida and my daughters, Emily and Erica, for their good-natured tolerance of "my writing state," that irritable energy that excludes the people closest to you for a finite time so that you can reach out to total strangers.

Toronto, Canada

Preface

Many people want to write. Some to express themselves, others to reach out to other people—to move them to laughter or tears.

This book is written for those who want to write for radio and television, both media that reach out to many people. Radio and television are the key mass media of this century, and to be a writer in either medium implies power.

It is exciting, it is important; writing can be poetic, funny, sad, energetic. Writing for radio and television holds endless creative possibilities.

In order to write for these media, you have to understand how to best communicate in each medium. Each medium has its own techniques and formats. Writing in each means acknowledging in your writing both the limits and potential of each medium.

This is the main order of business of this book—to teach you how to write for each medium.

To do so means to deal with drama. How do you dramatize your idea? How do you use character? What do those characters say? Dialogue, character, conflict, these will become terms that can't be overused if you are to learn how to write. And what is the balance between information and emotion that is most appropriate for your story?

This book deals with radio and television not only because radio and television are the central means of mass communication but also because writers who prepare for television only lose a crucial experience.

Radio, of course, is heard only. Consequently the writer has to capture the listener by the most imaginative means possible. Using only language, sound effects, and music, the writer and producer create a world. The television writer of course has the additional visual opportunity. But as creative as television is, writers too often ignore the richness of language that made radio so important in our culture. It's the difference between watching a pratfall on television and anticipating the pratfall and its aftermath on radio; the first is straightforward, the second is fraught with opportunity for the radio writer. Both should make us laugh. But in radio there is that much more invention.

I know all of you would like to be well-paid writers. And I hope you will be. But imagine the satisfaction of inventing that pratfall for radio.

You smile! You can make us laugh or cry. You have a tremendous power as a writer—you can communicate, you can reach out and affect people in your community and in your society. And if you are very creative, you can reach out with written material that will still make people laugh or cry in 5 years time; perhaps even 50 years. This is the true power and influence of the writer.

Good luck and I hope this book will help you become what you want to become.

1

The Medium Forms the Message

Writers are storytellers. Writers for radio or television tell stories in a form that is suitable for those media. But they are also part of a large, creative, corporate industry that today is one of the largest and most important export industries in the United States (including the movie and television industries).

To work in that industry, the writer should know about that industry. How it is structured and how it works. In this chapter, I will begin with the industry and conclude with what it is that you write.

THE MEDIUM

Both radio and television are organized on similar lines. They can operate at the local community level where they relate to specific community programming needs, or they can operate at the national level. All radio and television stations are licensed by the Federal authority. And whether they deliver programming by radio or television signal, operate on the AM or FM band, or deliver service by cable, that programming would not exist if there were not a market for it.

Consequently, many radio and television stations specialize. There are stations devoted to music programming, or to talk shows, or to sports, or public affairs, or information, or movies or children's programs or to ethical television or to adult television.

With the advent of cable television, television viewers now have what radio listeners have enjoyed for many years—options.

Although radio tends to be more specialized than television, television is moving in the direction of increasing specialization. And as the television audience fragments, we are seeing channels devoted to high culture and to low culture. Network television of course is a mix—high culture, middle culture, sports, information and entertainment, where possible presented in as entertaining a fashion as possible.

Funding for radio and television is a mix of advertising revenue and program sales revenue. In the case of public radio and television, revenue is based on a mix of government grants, subscriber revenue, and donations. In the case of cable channels revenue is based on subscription revenue.

In all cases revenue needs and the fickleness of audiences keeps radio and television executives at local and national levels sensitive to their market. This pressure always translates into a demand for good writers and producers.

In radio and television there are never enough good writers or producers!

THE WRITER

So where does the writer fit into all of this?

Both radio and television are technical mediums that employ a broad range of technicians. It is best to think of the writer as the person who does the majority of his or her work before any of the technicians are necessary.

The production of a program for radio or television can be broken down into three phases—preproduction, production, and post-production.

In the first phase, preproduction, a producer works with a writer to develop an idea into a script suitable for production. Suitable means as many drafts as time and contractual obligations will tolerate. A script is never really finished. It's just time to go into production. So the writer stops and the actor arrives, or the journalist/reporter leaves for the location. This preproduction phase is the primary phase for the writer.

The production phase often relies on actors, sound technicians, and videographers or film cameramen as well as floor directors, production managers, and lots of assistants. The key carryover person from preproduction is the producer, who works continually through all the phases.

In the production stage, the writer may be called upon for additional rewrites. Particularly in network situation comedy, writers working with story editors and producers will do rewrites through rehearsals until the final taping. It is not uncommon, however, for the writer to have no role in this stage of production.

Post-production is the editing stage where the material is put together for broadcast. Sound effects, music, redubbing of a blown line of dialogue, are all added at this stage.

In the area of documentary, radio and television, there is an important role for the writer at this stage. The preparation of narration is only appropriate once the writer sees the visual material. The writing of narration is an important role for the writer but it is also a specialized role, only appropriate in particular types of productions, most often documentary.

The writer then is most important in the preproduction stage, the stage where the idea gets translated into script.

There are many more areas of radio and television that require writers than you might realize and they are worth mentioning here. The obvious jobs for writers are the entertainment sector of the industry from "Mary Tyler Moore" to "Miami Vice." This is only the tip of the employment iceberg.

Somebody has to write the evening news. And somebody else has to write those bad jokes you hear every morning listening to your favorite disc jockey. And somebody has to write those clever commercials that make us chuckle all the way to the store.

In fact, everything you hear on radio and see on television whether it be information or entertainment programming is written by a writer.

And not every writer continues to write for the same medium. Paddy Chayefsky began in radio and moved into television drama. Eventually he wrote movies. And then he produced and wrote movies. He even wrote a novel (*Altered States*) which he then converted into a screenplay. He even produced the movie.

Rod Serling was a writer, a producer; indeed with "Twilight Zone" he became the star of his own series, introducing a show as evocatively as Alfred Hitchcock.

James Brooks began as a television writer. Then he wrote and produced the "Mary Tyler Moore Show." And then he wrote, produced, and directed *Terms of Endearment*. He is now an important writer, producer, and director.

William Goldman is a novelist and a screenwriter (*Marathon Man*). Harold Pinter has written for radio, television, theater, and the movies. And then there is Woody Allen!

Writers don't stay in one place. Just as they are creative in their writing, they can be creative in their careers.

One cliché that is continually being reverified in radio and television is that there is only one limit to your career—talent. With a little luck, talented writers have gone far. With a lot of luck, less talented writers have gone far. There is no simple pattern for writers.

THE MESSAGE

The writer, whether writing a commercial, a miniseries, or a radio documentary, will take into account the many factors that will make his or her written script most effective.

In order to understand those many factors it is best to start with the general and then to become more specific. Many of the general themes here mentioned will be brought up repeatedly. They are important.

THE AUDIENCE

Who are you writing for?

Is it a specialized audience or is it the widest possible audience? You would not write the same show about heart attack for a class of medical students as you would for the general public.

Is there an age factor involved?

This is particularly important in the area of family drama. An adult treatment of your subject would not be suitable in a family drama where teenagers and their parents are your primary audience.

Is there a cultural factor involved?

If your show is primarily intended for international television, will it be understood in other cultures? If the story is about a particular culture, have you, the writer, informed yourself fully about that culture? If you have, the result is likely to be credible. If not, the story will be overly stereotyped and potentially offensive.

Is there a regional factor involved?

If your story is region-specific or community-specific, has it been written in the idiom/style/content meaningful to that region or community?

Is your audience expecting entertainment or information? Or both?

What a writer writes will be affected by all these audience considerations. To ignore who your audience is, imperils the effectiveness of your story and certainly has dire consequences for your career.

THE GOAL

Beyond reaching an audience, the writer wants to achieve a particular goal in the production of his or her efforts. The writer of a commercial wants the viewer to buy a particular product. The writer of a miniseries wants the viewer to be vastly entertained. The writer of a radio documentary may want the listener to be moved to social action.

Whether the goal is entertainment or social action, the writer applies his or her skills and creativity to achieve that goal. Together with considerations of who the audience is, the writer can work to achieve that goal. If the writer does, he or she is successful.

DRAMATIC VALUES

A slice of life is a slice of life. A dramatized slice of life will be a good radio or television drama.

Drama means, in brief, conflict. A person in conflict with another person or with a community or with himself. Conflict and a conflicted character raise the inevitable question. Will the person get out of trouble? Our desire to see the person get out of trouble as well as our identification with that person or with their situation are necessary ingredients to get us involved with the story.

The story itself can be about anything. A critical point in my life, a central event in a community, a historical event. The story can be imaginary or based on real events.

But in all cases how the story is told has to be strong on dramatic values. Conflict and character are central to the creation of dramatic values.

ENERGY

Storytelling for radio and television works when we are involved and unaware of technique. In part, this comes from dramatic values, particularly our identification with the character or situation. But it also comes from the level of energy in the storytelling.

Characters acting out of a sense of urgency are more involving than pliant or passive characters. In fact, it is difficult to remain involved with passive or constantly agreeable characters. Resistance, reaction, and moving towards a goal requires considerable assertion from characters. This motion generates a sense of urgency that energizes a story.

In order to stay involved in a story, a great deal of energy is necessary. Just as in life we find ourselves attracted to people who are energetic, we are also attracted to stories that give off energy. But unlike real life, listening to radio or watching television is a solitary experience. And since its easy to turn off the radio or switch the television channel, the energy on that screen together with our involvement with the dramatic values of the story has to keep us from turning off the radio or switching off the channel.

IMMEDIACY

Some viewers or listeners prefer to escape from the everyday issues that barrage them in the newspapers or in their daily lives. Fantasy and wish fulfillment are their goals in listening and viewing.

Most viewers and listeners, however, expect a relationship between what they listen to or watch and their lives and communities. Consequently, the success of "60 Minutes," the miniseries "Roots," or the television series "Cheers" has everything to do with how those programs and their subject matter touches the lives of audiences.

The issues, whether they be controversial (the quality of North American education), or noncontroversial (the family unit is desirable again), are the subject matter of radio and television.

The more an issue or personality is in the news, the more likely the public appetite for material about that person or event. Few media are more responsive to issues of the day than radio or television. And as viewpoints about those issues change over time, those changes are quickly reflected in television series and radio talk shows.

How many television shows have you seen recently about ecological issues? You didn't see shows about ecology five years ago. This has everything to do with public consciousness. And writers, as antennae for those developments in public consciousness and public anxiety, know that stories about these issues will appeal to viewers and listeners.

Even if the treatment of the story is fantasy-oriented or rife with wish-fulfillment, the subject matter has an urgency, an immediacy for audiences, and consequently, both sober documentaries and fantastic optimistic treatments of these stories will find their audiences.

Writers should be aware of the type of subject matter that has this immediacy.

IMAGINATION

We live in a world inundated with information, things, ideas, movements. And it's all moving so quickly that it's very easy to turn off from that flood. The consequence is to see the world in a controlled, stereotypical construct. Since each of us is the gatekeeper of what and who we let into our lives, it is easy to fall into this guarded position. It gives us a sense of control over our lives.

Viewers, listeners, and writers are all susceptible to this position.

But when we are alone listening to the radio or watching television (even with others in the room, we relate to that little orbit box) something special can happen.

Because we relate to the audio or audiovisual material on a one-to-one basis, the writer and producer of that material can reach us without the intrusion if we wish (we usually do) of phone calls, demands from family and work, from bankers and lawyers. The result is an openness to stimulation, an openness we too often discard in everyday modern life.

The result is an enormous opportunity for what is best described as relatedness and the sense of a new experience. The quality of that new experience will be directly affected by the creativity of the writer and producer of the radio or television program being watched.

The imagination of the writer here is critical. Recognizable people experiencing surprise, new insights, new situations, new opportunities, make us smile and sometimes laugh or cry. This imaginative energized experience when we have it on radio or television is not only reassuring to audiences, it is positively stimulating. And the result is a devotion to programs that is quite remarkable.

I know more than one person for whom watching "thirtysomething" is more important than the daily news or calling their mother every Tuesday. This type of devotion is the result of imagination, the audience's need for this kind of stimulation and the writer's creative investment.

The more imagination a program exhibits, the greater that devotion. It's a considerable responsibility for the writer for radio and television. But it is also a great opportunity.

LANGUAGE

Writers inevitably have to rely on language to communicate with audiences. Their stories can have dramatic values, energy, and immediacy. They can be imaginatively told. But in the end the characters, the reporters, the talk show hosts and the baby food salespersons speak.

What they say, how they say it, can either ruin all the good efforts put into the development of your story so far, or it can help you reach new heights.

Radio particularly depends almost exclusively on language. But in many ways so does television.

In language we look first for recognizability. Does it seem believable? But beyond believability we look for surprise. Whether it be a surprising laugh in a situation comedy or a poetic observation in a documentary, language should surprise us and it should stimulate us.

I will return to this issue of language in Chapter 5 but it is important for you to realize that what people say in your story will be important in the success of your radio drama or teleplay.

HOW THE MEDIUM FORMS THE MESSAGE

Which medium you work in will influence the degree to which you use language or immediacy and how you deploy dramatic values.

Radio

Radio is a medium of language and imagination and immediacy.

Although there are radio plays that are based upon classic novels or plays set in the past or future, the majority of radio work is closely related to what is happening in the community or society today. Personal, social, and political issues, both national and international, dominate local radio stations; the point of view, however, is based on its community. Consequently, the focus, the audience, and the writer's goals are quite specific.

Writing for radio generally is, on one level, very specific. Every entrance in a radio play begs the question, who is coming in, why, and where are they going? Because we can't see, we have to be led through the story with sound and dialogue.

This is a highly simplified but critical task for the writer and it is crucial in order to make sure the listener isn't lost.

A primary function of the reporter or narrator in the radio documentary is to ensure the listener doesn't get lost. The reporter or narrator becomes our guide.

But this is where the limit on radio ends. As long as the listener isn't lost, the writer can create the Battle of Borodino in *War and Peace* on radio. Properly set up and creatively using sound and dialogue, the writer can create this critical Napoleonic battle. And, if successful, it will be alive in the listener's imagination.

Dramatic values must be carefully simplified so that the listener can follow the action. But then the writer's use of sound effects and language is comparatively open-ended in radio. In fact, there has to be an over-reliance upon sound and language in radio. That's the nature of this medium.

Understanding these operating principles can give you tremendous freedom in the creation of a radio play or radio documentary.

Television

Television also thrives on immediacy but as a visual medium; the writer has to conform to the economic as well as the visual realities of a production. In short, it would be very difficult for any television program but the most expensive miniseries to produce Tolstoy's *War and Peace*. As mentioned previously, such a project is eminently producible on radio.

The writer for television has to consider the full gamut of economic considerations.

Is the show part of a series? How long is the production period for the show? If production requires a shorter shooting schedule, a complex story with numerous locations may be impractical. Is the show produced on location or in studio? This factor also will limit the number of characters and locations in the teleplay.

Economic factors can never be ignored by the television writer.

The next factor crucial to the writer is to present his or her story in keeping with the style/content of the series, whether it be drama or documentary.

Most television series and miniseries will produce a "bible" or guidebook for the writer which will set the style/content pattern for the teleplay.

Familiarity with the nature of continuing characters as well as the philosophy of the show will assure the writer's teleplay conforms to the producer's expectations.

Within these specific constraints the writer is free to be creative with his or her stories. Immediacy, imagination, energy, and dramatic values are all critical to the continuing success of any television show or series.

To ignore economic or producer expectations is to consign oneself to the lonely life of the poet far from the field of television.

In both radio and television the medium forms the message. The intermediary is the producer. But it is the writer who does the translating of the message for the medium.

Now that you know in what way you are important, let's move on to where you will find your stories.

2

▼
▼
▼
▼
▼

How to Find Your Story

To find a good story for radio and television, the first step is to know what you are looking for.

I have already suggested that good stories have particular qualities—energy, immediacy, and dramatic values. It is time to get more specific.

Both radio and television thrive on human interest stories. Even revolutions and wars, when they are the subject matter, are presented in the most personal terms. A good recent example is the 30-hour miniseries, "War and Remembrance." The history of World War II is told through the experiences of the members of one family.

The key to good stories is character. An unusual character in a conventional situation or a usual character in an unconventional situation, both have the seeds of good stories. That human element is what brings us into your story. The first test of a good story is do you have a good character?

The second test of a good story is the situation. A once prosperous town is about to become a ghost town. The last occupant is leaving today. His great-grandfather owned many of the industries in this town. He was born here. And today is his last day in the town that has been his home.

Or a student rushes home with the good news: She has been accepted to medical school. In the excitement she has forgotten. She hands her father her acceptance. But he can't read. He is illiterate. In that instant a greater chasm than ever exists between daughter and father.

Both situations, the end of a town and the end of a particular relationship, are rich in two qualities—crisis and conflict. Good stories for radio and television take place in situations that have lots of conflict.

THE USEFULNESS OF POLARITIES

Conflict doesn't have to be translated exclusively as a variation on the gunfight at the OK Corral. All of us find ourselves in conflict-laden circumstances quite often. Disagreements, of a wide variety of sorts and at all levels of society, have made the legal profession one of the most important in our society.

Conflict is very useful for telling good stories. But a more specific technique you can use to create conflict within your story is the use of polarities or extreme opposites. Good stories if you are looking for them, have a lot of polarities.

Stories about marriages between members of different religions, or cultures, or races, have this principle of opposites operating. One can almost imagine how the in-laws, brothers, or bosses react. Stories set in schools where students and teachers occupy opposite power positions and stories set in hospitals where patients and doctors occupy opposite power and wellness-illness positions are useful examples of settings where polarities are at play.

We can use polarities in character, the young and the old, the rich and the poor, the stable and the unstable, the white and the black; the possibilities for polarities are endless. A good story for radio and television will have polarities in character.

And that story will probably also have polarities operating in the situation. American soldiers in Viet Nam, a young woman away from home for the first time, a famous television reporter involved in his or her first meaningful personal relationship, all of these situations exhibit the principle of polarities.

Good stories have lots of polarities in character and situation.

So far, good stories have characters we can get involved with in interesting situations. There are lots of polarities in the character and in the situation, and the story should have energy and immediacy. Now let's get more specific about the type of stories you should be looking for.

THE PERSONAL STORY

The personal story can be biographical or it can be intimate and shorter in time frame. In both cases the focal point of the story is an individual whose circumstances or experiences are unusual or important. In all cases the focus is on the human dimension of the character.

Whether it is a story about George Patton or Dr. Fredrick Banting, these stories focus less on the historical importance of the character. Their histories form the background of the story.

In the foreground, the story focuses on George Patton as father or Banting as husband.

Personal stories can be about families or they can be about individuals. A story about Van Gogh's emotional turmoil focuses more on the failure of relationships and his resulting loneliness; his story as an artist remaining in the background.

Personal stories tend to focus on a significant period or event in the character's life. Paddy Chayefsky's *Marty* focuses on an aging bachelor's first significant relationship with a woman. Rod Serling's *Requiem for a Heavyweight* focuses on the end of a boxer's career. Births and deaths are the most significant events and, in between, leaving home, forming new relationships, establishing a new home, all are as significant dramatically as they are in real life.

So, too, are the highs and lows of life. Achievement, failure, health, illness, wealth, poverty, all of these states and how a character deals with them often form the subject matter of the personal story.

The personal story is told in close and, consequently, there is a sense of intimacy with the character that is more emotional than the more distanced kind of approach. As a result the sense of judgement we as viewers and listeners can formulate when watching or listening to this kind of story treatment means a powerful sense of identification with the character. There is room for little else in the personal story. But the reward is an intensity unavailable to the writer of other types of stories.

THE FAMILIAR STORY

There are stories that are perennials. The principal virtue is that they are immediately recognizable to the audience. The secret for the writer is to find a new twist in the familiar story. That new twist makes it seem fresh and may be related to a particular point of view prevalent in the contemporary society.

Familiar stories include the teenage rebellion, first love, the lottery win, the failure of the family farm. Variations on these stories are lifted from the headlines on page one of the newspaper. In the fifties a story about teenage rebellion might take the point of view that the society as a whole was too controlling, too intolerant of individual differences. In the sixties, stories of teenage rebellion took the form of celebrations of freedom. In the seventies, such stories became stories of rites of passage (as if teenage rebellion were not only expected but also respected). In the eighties, stories of teenage rebellion are presented as romantic echoes of simpler times (there is nostalgia here totally absent from the fifties stories).

The benefit for the radio and television writer is that these stories are almost formulaic in structure. All the writer has to do is to develop interesting characters and discover that contemporary twist that will make the familiar story seem fresh.

THE ORIGINAL STORY

The original story is exactly the opposite of the familiar story. Almost everything, character and situation, surprises us. If there is any familiarity, it is token.

Perhaps the most famous original radio show was Orson Welles' "War of the Worlds." This dramatized version of an invasion of the United States by extraterrestrials was so realistic (it was broadcast as if the nightly news had just been interrupted by a national emergency) that many listeners panicked in the belief that an invasion was actually underway.

One of the most original television shows was "The Fugitive." A man is on the run. He gets involved with people but never for more than an episode. He has to elude his pursuer. This series about a man who couldn't put down roots, was free to allow the character to roam into situations or into the lives of other characters. Nothing but the pursuit and the main character's amnesia remained from week to week. All other story elements were ever-changing.

The original story for radio and television is compelling but the exception. As a result, it is more difficult to sell and produce. These stories always require an aggressive style ("The Prisoner," "War of the Worlds") or a concept that grabs the imagination and won't seem to let go ("The Fugitive").

When you are looking for a story you will recognize the original story idea. It is not quite like anything you've experienced. And it has caught your imagination.

Needless to say, these stories are rare. So if you are struck with the above feelings too often, it is no longer original.

THE CLASSIC STORY

There is a type of story that, for lack of a better term, I am calling the classic story. In theme, these stories are reminiscent of the great literature you had to read in high school.

We could pause for a moment to consider what constitutes great—is it the scope of the character? Is it the scale of the situation the character finds himself in? Probably both. But it has to be more. From a story point of view, all classic stories are making a statement about morality. Macbeth is so ambitious and so blinded by his ambitions, that he becomes a murderer. Romeo and Juliet's love is destroyed by the hatred their families have for one another. Willlie Loman's lie to his son Biff in *Death of a Salesman* is symptomatic of a man who has spent his life lying to others and to himself. In the end the lie kills him.

In this sense, the classic story tells a story but it also teaches us something about life.

These classic stories intertwine the lives of characters with the societies of the day. And as we read these stories we realize that the stories recur, because they have meaning to people throughout the ages.

Stories of the prodigal son (*Bus Riley's Back in Town*), rivalrous brothers (*East of Eden*), destructive marriages (*Who's Afraid of Virginia Woolf*), intergenerational strife (*I Never Sang for My Father*), unbridled ambition (*Wall Street*) or messianic con artists (*Elmer Gantry*) become radio or television stories generation after generation.

The names may be different, there may be modifications in the situation, and they may take place today rather than in the era of the original, but these stories are classic. They can be retold again and again and the audience will relate to them. Witness the 1962 remake of *Romeo and Juliet*. *West Side Story* is set to music in contemporary New York. Instead of the Italian Montagues and the Capulets, we have two street gangs. Their hatred for each other kills the modern Romeo and Juliet. But our memory of the strength of the idealistic love lives on.

Classic stories are a great source of material for radio and television.

WHERE TO FIND STORIES

Writers use their dreams or the daily newspaper when faced with coming up with a story. But you don't have to restrict yourself.

Whether you believe newspapers report the news or make the news, you can take advantage of the wide variety of papers available. Differing political perspectives, hard news, soft news, all is grist for your mill. Newspapers, because they have to capture your attention and keep your loyalty as a reader, tell their stories in a particular way. They highlight the drama in a news story and they report in a concise, to the point, manner. You are left with "the meat" of the story. In this sense newspapers are important source material. They also tell you what is in style, issue-wise.

After newspapers, magazines, particularly political and lifestyle magazines; both are caught up in locating the next issue of importance.

It is fine to use newspapers and magazines to find ideas and issues for stories, but we should distinguish particularly with regards to magazines that you can't simply use a magazine article as the basis of your radio or television story. You can't unless you buy the right to do so.

Magazines, books, radio and television programs, movies are all subject to copyright laws (as are newspapers). The result is that unless you have an agreement with the copyright owner (publisher, producer, production company, radio station), you cannot adapt that work and make it your own.

Consequently, you can only use newspapers and magazines or any copyright material to give you a sense of the issues of the day, or the seed of an idea. You cannot literally transfer at will material from a newspaper or book to your story unless that material is in the public domain.

Newspaper reporting about public figures is information in the public domain. Adaptations of books whose copyright has lapsed are also material in the public domain. Copyright is registered in the country of origin; depending on the country this means a copyright for 50–100 years. Copyrights are renewable. In doubt, you should seek out information about copyright. This information is available through a lawyer. Copyright ownership is listed inside all publications.

I mention newspapers and magazines because familiarity with them will tell you what media people think are important human interest and social interest issues of the day. They also communicate in their reportage and how they write it, the viewpoint on particular issues. This is important because radio and television are not radical media. They like to be on the edge of issues but not ahead of that edge.

You should also watch television and listen to the radio. Together with newspaper and magazine input, you will have a fairly good sense of what is making news and what is being made into programming. Your good idea may come directly from you reading, listening, and watching. Or it may come in reaction to what you're reading, listening to, and watching.

You may decide to adapt a song into a screen story as Arlo Guthrie did in *Alice's Restaurant*. Or you may find your inspiration in that endearing tale of self-sacrifice *A Tale of Two Cities*. Adaptation as long as you clarify the copyright problem, is an excellent source of material. You've got a great character or characters. And you've got a gripping situation. All you have to do is make the story meaningful for today's audience. That's what Francis Ford Coppola did in *Apocalypse Now*. He set Joseph Conrad's *Heart of Darkness* in Viet Nam in 1968 instead of Africa at the turn of the century. The key is to make the story relevant to today's audience.

What I haven't talked about yet is the source of many radio and television stories—personal observations. Writers should be observant and when they are they see the idiosyncrasies going on all around them. You can see whole stories or you can use a fragment, something observed, to build up a story.

Personal observation for a writer should include the self. Very often our own experiences can be the basis of excellent stories. Whether it is a person you have loved or hated, an experience that was memorable, or how you dealt or didn't deal with a personal crisis, all is filtered through your own eyes. This can make it different from all the other stories about like experiences and people.

Trust your instincts. If you have been gripped by an experience, if you tell the story right, we will be gripped, too.

Research vs. Imagination

When you are assessing a story for its possibilities for a broadcast medium, you should also assess how you are going to flesh out the story. Is it a story that requires a lot of hard information? Or is it a story that can be created out of your imagination? If it is a story that needs a lot of research, can you find the necessary information? If so, where do you find it?

If it is a story with imaginative possibilities, is that option within your capacities?

In both cases time frame should play a role in your assessment. Stories, particularly that derive from the news, have a finite shelf life. You don't want a story that will be yesterday's news by the time you've finished your research. Both documentary and dramatic material require research. But dramatic material is, relatively speaking, more reliant on your imagination.

Research Techniques

Once you have decided upon your story, you should make yourself as familiar as possible with background material. If you are writing a script about the common cold, you should make yourself as familiar as possible with the subject. The writer's task is to become an almost instant expert on the subject of the common cold.

To do so you can use primary as well as secondary sources.

Primary information is first hand. Primary sources include doctors, nurses, people with colds, as well as all direct observation you undertake.

Secondary sources include articles, books, films about the common cold.

Generally documentaries for radio and television cannot be enriched enough by secondary research.

Primary sources usually yield the anecdotes; the firsthand interview material with doctors and patients that will humanize your documentary.

The closer you get to your subject, the more likely you'll get interesting information that in turn will make your script better. This, too, points to primary sources over secondary sources.

Dramatic material also implies research. To write *Rain Man*, the writer had to familiarize himself with autism. There are many books and articles on the subject. But to create the drama, he also had to go into hospitals and sheltered halfway houses to observe the behavior of the autistic person. Without this research, the script could not have been written.

In order to undertake your research an audio tape recorder is indispensable. When you talk to people about your subject, you want information. But you have to realize that if you are doing research for a radio documentary or for TV, you may very well be auditioning an individual for the show. Consequently, you want a record of the information, but also want to assess the delivery of that information.

To do so, you have to establish a rapport with the person you are interviewing. It is your responsibility to make them comfortable enough to:

1. Share information.
2. Offer opinions.
3. Tell you anecdotes that might be useful to humanize the material.
4. Establish a presence that you can assess in terms of its effectiveness for the radio or TV show.

It is hard to do all this when you are writing notes. It is easier if you are tape recording the interview: Understandably, you can only tape them if they agree. If they don't you will have to settle for a writing pad.

Just as you can yield valuable information from interviewing people, your script can benefit considerably from on site visits and observation sessions. If your story takes place in an institution, the fabric of life in that institution will only become apparent if you are around, watching, waiting, recording. A sense of the place will affect your story. So plan to hang around wherever your show is to take place.

To reiterate, interview and observe.

You will need equipment; in most cases a tape recorder. If people and budget permit, video recording can be very helpful. One note of caution. Video recorders in a research situation can be viewed as very intrusive. You may get information but it may not be very viable.

People are better interview subjects when:

1. They are an integral part of the story.
2. They are comfortable with you.

A calm, professional demeanor together with respect for them as a person or as a professional will go a long way to helping you get the type of information most useful for the script.

You're almost ready to begin shaping your material into a script. But before you do, make sure how you feel about this story. Whether it is familiar, personal, or classic, your commitment to the story has to be considerable.

If it is not, you'll end up with a flat script. If you are excited or feel strongly about the subject, a more energetic treatment is likely.

One final comment. Some ideas are better than others for broadcast material. Issues of the day are always strong. So are unusual human interest stories. So, too, are stories that take a stand on a controversial issue. And then there are the classics—those universal stories that get retold in every generation. If your story is one of the above, you are on the right track.

Now, on to how to tell your story.

3

How to Tell Your Story

All stories can be enhanced in the telling. They can also be undermined. It is the old adage of never beginning a joke with a punch line.

In order to tell your story effectively, whether for radio or television, technique is critical. Those techniques are the subject matter of this chapter.

BEGINNINGS

Openings are crucial. They can and should capture our interest. And they should let us know what the story will be about and who will be our guide (narrator in documentary or main character in drama). An example will be helpful.

The story is about a librarian who decides she can be an important politician and runs for political office. In the course of the story she becomes that important politician.

Since the librarian's task seems almost impossible, there appears to be lots of latitude for conflict.

In order to capture the improbability as well as the desire, one opening that would serve the drama would be as follows:

A devoted librarian receives a layoff slip. She is so outraged that she writes a note to the mayor. We don't quite see what she has written. After finishing the note, she personally delivers it to the mayor's office.

The mayor's assistant reads the note. He laughs. He can't help himself. He takes it into the mayor's office. The librarian remains outside. A moment later, laughter emanates from the mayor's interior office. She is certain she will have the last laugh at the mayor's expense.

THE MOMENT

You should try to join your story at a highly dramatic moment. Too often stories resemble diaries; they tell the story of a character, of a relationship or of an event. And they tell the story from its beginning to end. Time is spent introducing the character, evolving the relationship, and explaining the genesis of the event.

If you are too expository at the beginning, the audience may have left by the time you get around to a dramatic incident in your story.

Finding the moment to join your story is one of your most crucial decisions. If we join the action in midstream, with the characters perplexed about how to deal with their situation, we are in the middle of the dramatic situation. This is a much more exciting beginning than the slow explanatory route.

If you pick the moment right, the energy level or urgency will help carry the viewer or listener into the story and assure their rapt attention and craving to know what will happen next.

STRUCTURE

Radio and television stories are presented in three phases: The *setup*, the *struggle*, and the *resolution*.

Each phase has dramatic values, conflict, but how that conflict is deployed escalates through the phases.

In the first phase, the setup, the character and the situations are introduced. The problem for the character is highlighted in a way that emphasizes to us the magnitude of the problem.

In the example I used, the librarian is introduced. Her problem is that she is being put out of her job. She blames the politicians in the mayor's office. And she lets them know.

In the second phase, the struggle, the librarian struggles to become a politician herself. Some people may help her. Others will hinder her.

In phase three, the resolution, she does become a politician. What this means for her personal and professional life is part of the resolution.

THE PLOT

The action of the story is called the plot. Particular types of stories require elaborate plotting, with frequent twists and turns. Other stories which rely more heavily on character have less plot.

Today's audiences however, whether watching a television drama or listening to a radio documentary, are accustomed to a great deal of plot.

Just as commercials have moved toward elaborate 30- or 60-second narratives, so, too, have television and, to a relative degree, radio.

A question you can't ask yourself enough is whether your story has sufficient plot.

SURPRISE

The twists and turns of the story introduce the elements of surprise into the story. Audiences like to be swept up by surprise in a story. It is the equivalent of the downturn on the roller coaster. We're afraid of it, but we're excited by it. So, too, should we be by your story.

CHARACTER

It is important to the story that we empathize with the main character. Generally we identify with the main character and live through the challenges with that character.

Identification, or at the very least, empathy is critical. Without it we remain outside the story.

This issue is so important that we will devote a chapter to it.

CONFLICT

The nature of drama is conflict. It is a crucial dimension of documentary and drama, radio and television.

How to create conflict in your story is not as difficult as you might imagine.

In police stories the source of conflict is always criminal activity in the face of the law. This is an obvious form of conflict. Less obvious but no less important is the emotional conflict characters face when making a decision.

An adult cares for his elderly father who is increasingly unable to care for himself. Should he put his father in a nursing home or should he try to keep him at home in spite of the next to impossible circumstances? This type of emotional conflict is also crucial in storytelling. Often it's more effective than the more obvious criminal vs. police conflict.

Conflict can arise out of any situation. What is important for the storyteller is that the type of conflict you use in the first phase of your teleplay is different from the level of conflict you use in the final phase. As your story unfolds, the level of conflict should be rising. This means that more is at stake for your main character near the end of your story than in the early phase.

In this way, your story not only moves toward a resolution but, through that final conflict, your viewers or listeners experience the climax of the story and laugh or cry as you had hoped they would.

POLARITIES

The use of extreme opposites in character against character or character against situation is the mechanics of conflict. You can modulate these opposites for the degree of conflict. The principle of polarities will be very useful to you.

The helpless librarian and the powerful mayor is one polarity introduced at the beginning of this chapter.

THE CLIMAX

The end of your story is the critical determinant whether your audience feels satisfied or feels as you want them to feel at the end of your story.

Creating a proper climax requires that you examine once again why your character got into the dilemma he or she is in in the first place. What is the worst thing that can happen to them given what they want? If you know the answer, you've got the climax to your story.

DIALOGUE

What your characters say can help inform, amuse, engage, or outrage the listener or viewer.

Dialogue is sufficiently important that we will devote Chapter 5 to it.

ATMOSPHERE

Whether it is sound effects and music on radio, or the appearance of the environment, or the clothing of the characters, or even the posture of the characters, all of the above contribute to the atmosphere of the show.

You are telling a story but at one level that story, when produced, has to sound or look believable.

Your attention as a writer to the nonverbal elements of your story, the atmosphere, will determine whether the audience believes your story or not.

If they don't, you are in trouble.

Writers create atmosphere by the use of detail, relevant detail. The person in mourning, long after the death of a spouse, always in black clothing, the unmade bed, the attendance to pictures of the spouse, the visit to the grave of the spouse; all of these details may have nothing to do with the plot but they tell us a lot about the character. More important, together they make the character more believable, more real.

This type of attention to relevant detail around issues of location as well as character will create an atmosphere that contributes credibility to your story.

Your story may be fine without atmosphere but it will be positively gripping with the contribution it adds to your script.

Believability is a very important factor to how an audience will receive your material. Atmosphere will help you in the area of believability.

Before we turn to the evolution of script from idea to script it is useful to pose particular questions that should be uppermost in your mind as you write your script.

DOES YOUR STORY HAVE ENOUGH PLOT

Beyond the implicit question, is your story compelling? is the issue of plotting. Are there enough twists and turns in your script? Do you deploy surprise for impact?

Generally beginning writers do not employ enough plot.

Going on this assumption you can use particular devices to introduce more plot. All television shows use the strategy of more than one story line. In a half hour show it is typical to have a major story line and a minor story line. The two should have a link to one another.

A recent episode of "Dear John" had as the major story John's anniversary of his divorce. He is depressed and eating lots of Oreo cookies. How he will cope with the anniversary is of concern to him, as well as to his workshop friends.

The secondary story has to do with another anniversary. An elderly member of his group is having her 50th high school reunion. Since she is fearful she will see her former best friend, the woman who stole her fiancée, she is looking to make an impression.

The two stories come together when John becomes her date.

The use of major and minor stories is widely used in television. But some programs use more than two stories to make the show even more dynamic. Soap operas use as many as four stories intertwined in a 1-hour show. This principle was effectively adapted in "Hill Street Blues."

Again, the aim is to introduce sufficient plot to keep the audience interested and guessing. When you're writing your script consider whether your story has enough plot.

DO YOU HAVE ENOUGH EMOTION IN YOUR STORY

Inevitably how an audience feels about a show is determined by their emotional response to the main character and, to a lesser degree, to the other characters.

That emotion can be positive in relation to the main character and it can be negative in relation to the antagonist. Both are important.

Without the emotional connection, your story is in trouble.

What do I mean by emotion? Well, it is a wide term. It can mean tears about Snow White's fate or it can mean admiration for Lou Grant's stand on a particular issue. Or it can mean antagonism towards Darth Vader. The nature of the emotional response is less important than its presence.

Audiences engage with radio and television for information and entertainment. But, at the baseline, these media engage their audiences best when the emotional connection between audience and medium is present. Stories, whether for radio or television, work best when that emotional connection is present.

CHARACTER VS. PLOT

No matter how much plot is presented in a story, the absence of a character to care about will neutralize the impact of the plot. And conversely, the more radio time or television time spent on characterization, the less time there is for plot.

There appears to be a built-in trade-off between character and plot. For the maximum impact you need both. And yet you can't afford the time it takes to attend fully to both.

There are stories where you don't need both—the character-oriented story where there is less plot. These stories work best when the character is facing a deep personal crisis—the onset of a fatal disease to a family member, the displacement from a job held all one's working life. And there are plots that are so captivating that the stories can survive using the most quickly drawn, stereotypical characters.

In order to work with both, you will have to adopt particular shortcuts. Where plot and character are equally important, use only those aspects of characterization that relate directly to the plot.

Captain Call's stubbornness in "Lonesome Dove" leads to his decision to go on the cattle drive and later to return Augustus's body to Texas. Both actions in their scope, risk, and the outrageous odds against success, suggest a lot about Captain Call's character, but those decisions are also critical to the plot of "Lonesome Dove."

The message to the writer is clear. Scenes can serve and should serve more than one purpose; in the example above, the scenes characterize but also advance the plot.

Another shortcut is to vary the emphasis in your major and minor stories. If your major story is character-intensive, your minor story should be plot-intensive. In this way the differences will work in your favor in terms of the needs of the opposite story.

A third shortcut is the placement of characterization scenes. They should not take place throughout the radio or television story. Character-oriented scenes should be placed primarily in the first half of the radio play or teleplay. The second half should be given over to plot-oriented scenes. Indeed, as we move toward the end, the scenes should be virtually all plot-oriented.

Character and plot are competing needs within your story. You need them both but you should also be aware that you have to deploy each in ways that serve your story.

TENSION AND HUMOR

Media stories are intended to captivate and maintain the interest of the audience. As a result, you need a good story and you have to tell it on the assumption that the audience is fickle. They can turn you off at any point.

The problem of maintaining interest, then, is a constant concern for the writer and producer.

We have already discussed the usefulness for conflict situations and conflicted characters in telling your story. The result is tension in the telling of the story.

But it is difficult to maintain a constant escalation of tension in a story. To moderate that build of tension, humor is the most useful device. It also serves to charm the audience. The delicate balance between alarm and charm is a subtlety of technique that is very helpful to writers.

This relationship is not a secret to playwrights. Edward Albee's first act in *Who's Afraid of Virginia Woolf* is extremely funny. So, too, are the first 20 pages of Sam Shepherd's *Fool for Love*. But both plays are American tragedies. Rod Serling understood this relationship. So did Alfred Hitchcock.

How this operates in your stories should follow this pattern.

At a point in your story the buildup of tension may be difficult or beginning to stretch credibility. At such points, you should use humor. But to do so in a credible way here are some suggestions:

1. Have a character use humor to react to the tension in the scene, rather than make a joke or two that is unrelated to the situation.
2. If you designate a character who deals with all sorts of situations through humor, the introduction of humor will seem more natural. The purpose of tha character in your story might be solely for comic relief.
3. This type of humor usually is expressed verbally. Visual humor at this stage might make farcical all the dramatic values of the scene.
4. Be consistent in the type of humor used or the character who is humorous. Avoid each character taking turns being funny.

If you use humor to moderate the level of tension in your story, you will find that your story will be much more appealing to your audience.

HOW TO GET US MORE INVOLVED IN YOUR STORY

This section is actually a summary of a number of devices already mentioned. If you are concerned that we are not involved enough, use what follows as a checklist of devices.

Dramatic devices to increase involvement include:

1. An empathic main character
2. A compelling premise
3. A strong antagonist
4. An elaborate plot
5. A strong crisis point that begins your story
6. The use of surprise in your plotting
7. Emotional high points
8. A structure that escalates conflict in your story
9. The use of detail to enhance believability
10. The use of humor for charm and the modulation of tension

Writers for radio and television are always concerned to keep their audiences involved. The critical centrality of this problem suggests you can never have enough of the ten.

Realize, however, that you can modulate these factors. If, for example, you have a main character who is less than empathic, even bordering on disagreeable, all you have to do is put him or her in a situation where all the other characters are bordering on the despicable. Or put the main character in a situation where we would feel pressured, uncomfortable, fearful, and we will naturally feel empathic towards your main character. There is also the option of using an extremely hateful antagonist. The main idea is that there are trade-offs that can bring the same result—the viewer's involvement with your character and your story.

Now, in order to crystallize the evolution of an idea to a script, it would be useful to go through the stages as that idea evolves into a script. As it does, the individual factors such as characterization, conflict, and the plotting come into play.

A DIARY OF THE SCRIPT

You have an idea that you want to develop. That idea may be a character or incident, a headline or possibly a printed story. Whatever it is, the first likely exposure for a producer will be that idea packaged in the form of an outline.

THE OUTLINE

The outline of an idea is often no more than a few pages and can be as short as a few paragraphs.

The outline introduces a character and the problem that will face that character in the story. It will locate the action in time. An outline does not tell the plot line nor introduce all the characters.

If there is going to be more than one story line, however, it could allude to that fact through a description of another character and through his or her particular dilemma.

If the outline is part of a series, reference (through reading thc bible for that series) should be made to the continuing characters in the series and the dilemmas described should fit in attitude and approach into the philosophy of that particular series.

For example, the following is an outline for a story about second marriages.

John Smith and Mary Brown have decided to get married. They are each 45. They are each divorced with two to three grown children. Their children don't know each other because John and Mary have been very secretive.

The big night is tomorrow. The night before, they receive the surprise of their lives. His daughter and her son have been seeing each other. And they arrive together to tell each parent that they plan to marry. They are very surprised. They're all surprised. And some of them are not very happy about the surprise.

Will the Smiths and the Browns get together? Which ones will get together? To find out, stay tuned for the treatment.

Outlines tend to be to the point but not preachy; and they try to entertain and arouse curiosity in the reader.

THE TREATMENT

The treatment is an elaboration of the outline. The focus in that elaboration is the plot. The treatment is a scene by scene breakdown of the story.

It is at this point that the twists and turns of the story are decided upon. Each scene has a twist or turn. In essence each scene pushes the plot further down the road towards its climax.

Because all of the scenes are described in a paragraph, there isn't much more time than for the introduction of the various characters of the story. But that introduction should be more than in name.

For example, in a treatment of our John Smith - Mary Brown story, I would introduce them with a dominant characteristic. For instance, John Smith might be Dr. John Smith or the baseball player John Smith or the selfish John Smith. Mary Brown might be a company president or a social worker or the possessive Mary Brown. Similar types of description should encapsulate key characteristics for the kids. It is important that everybody be different than the others. Those differences will imply the reasons for the types of conflicts in which these people find themselves in the course of the story.

Generally treatment lengths depend upon the length of the show, the expectations of the producer, and the narrative purposes the treatment can serve for the writer. If the treatment is to be helpful to any of the above, try to write it in an energetic, lively manner. Too often treatments read as mechanical descriptions of character's movements through the story. If your approach is sterile, don't be surprised by a producer's response.

If, on the other hand, you use a vivid style, trying to help the producer or yourself as writer, pictorialize the story (even for radio!) you will find the language you choose will be more charged and the situations you create more focused for impact. The worst thing that can happen to a writer at this stage is the accusation of generality. This is the stage to focus your characters and your situations for impact. The treatment can be an important stage for the writer, but it can also pose problems. Different expectations in varying situations, working with different producers, suggest such a wide variety of expectations of the treatment stage, that this stage can be a minefield for writers. The best solution is to make your choices at this stage; be specific and be lively; producers need the reassurance and you need the work.

THE SCRIPT

The script is an elaboration of the treatment. The added features are dialogue and description in a drama and the narration in the documentary (if relevant). For radio, music references and sound effects would also be written in (where relevant).

This stage is not difficult, although dialogue always poses particular problems for many writers.

If your story has a focus, a point of view, and specific characters at the treatment stage, your script should follow; you might even feel free to enjoy the dialogue phase. If you enjoy it, so will the audience.

Remember that the script is a series of scenes. For television, you should think of every scene as crucial to the plot (a master scene rather than a transitional scene). On radio, because locating the action is important, you can use transitional scenes as well as master scenes.

Generally television scripts, depending on whether you use a film or video format, will be one to one and a half pages per minute of screen time. Radio scripts will run just over a page per minute. But variations in pace and the addition of sound effects and music will draw you closer to a page per minute.

In both cases we are talking about letter rather than legal size paper for the scripts.

THE SCENE

It would be useful to describe the writing of a scene to illustrate the types of choices you will face in your writing.

Every scene is self-contained. It exists for a specific purpose. Once that purpose is accomplished, the scene ends.

Every scene has to have tension or conflict. In order to create conflict in the scene, it is useful to give each character in the scene a goal. If there are two people, for example, in the scene, give them specific but opposite goals. When one of them achieves his goal (and the other doesn't) the scene is over, except for the need to set up the next scene.

The scene structure could be outlined as follows:

1. Introduction
2. Goal of character one
3. Goal of character two
4. Purpose of scene (plot-oriented)
5. Character one achieves goal
6. Introduction of location or character of the next scene (link to the next scene)

To illustrate how a scene would be developed, here is a scene from the outline I proposed earlier in this chapter.

In this scene, John Smith proposes marriage to Mary Brown:

```
THE SCENE: A nervous John Smith is making dinner for his
friend, Mary Brown. John is putting together a nice plate of
stuffed mushrooms. He arranges the plate to look as good as
possible.
     He enters the living room where Mary puts away her bifo-
cals. She is still embarrassed about needing them.
     He offers her an hors d'oeuvre.

                         MARY
     That's a neat set of mushrooms, John.

                         JOHN
     As long as they don't taste like golf balls.

                         MARY
     I'm so glad you made a fancy dinner tonight. I closed the
     deal of my career, I'm with the man in my life—if the kid's
```

were here the evening would be perfect.

                         JOHN
I'd like to meet your kids.

                         MARY
I told you not to mention that again. I'm just too guilty.

                         JOHN
What if we were to get married?

                         MARY
You're just saying that.

                         JOHN
No, I mean it. I wouldn't have made so many mushrooms if I
didn't mean it.

Mary begins to cry.

                         MARY
I feel so bad. I'm really happy!

                         JOHN

Which?

                         MARY

Both!

                         JOHN

Is that a yes?

                         MARY

Maybe.

                         JOHN
If it is a yes I could meet Larryand Michael, couldn't I?

                         MARY
I guess so.
John and Mary embrace.

In this scene:

1. The two characters are introduced having a romantic dinner alone.
2. John's goal is to propose.
3. Mary's goal is to keep her two lives separate; to keep John and her sons apart.
4. The purpose of the scene is to have John propose to Mary.
5. John has achieved his goal. It looks like Mary is accepting him.
6. The people introduced at the end of the scene, Larry and Michael, will ap
   pear in the next scene.

Remember that scenes have a purpose; they have a beginning, middle, and end; and the characters in the scene have different goals. When one character achieves his or her goal the scene is almost over. All that remains is the set-up for the next scene.

Now let's move on to an important subject for all writers—the characters in your story.

4

▼ Character Is Critical
▼ to Your Story

The first problem the writer faces about character is who are the people who should populate your story? How many of them should there be? And what aspect of their character will help your story?

As a writer you have to develop characters on paper who are recognizable and believable.

Who the character is and how to use that character effectively is the subject of this chapter.

DEVELOPING CHARACTERS

One of the most difficult aspects of writing, particularly for starting writers, is character development. Should you think of a movie or television star or a person you know? This is a question I'm asked all the time. My answer is, If it helps.

But for those of us who want to avoid using Dustin Hoffman one more time, it is useful to begin with purpose. What is the purpose of your character in the story? The people who populate your story should have a specific purpose.

Intentional Characters

People serve specific functions in a story. And that function relates to the nature of the conflicts in your story. If your story is about the dutiful son who always makes the choice for his family rather than himself, you need a character who is not selfish, who has dreams but no opportunity for explorations of those dreams. What this character does with his frustration is important to the drama. In Frank Capra's classic *It's a Wonderful Life*, this character turns his frustration on his wife and children and finally upon himself.

It is critical that our character not be self-absorbed or an adventurer. Either characteristic in our main character would undermine his dilemma. He has to be a man in the middle of a conflict and it is his character or nature that puts him there.

When we look at secondary characters in this story we can find the extremely selfish and we can find adventurers. Their function in the story is to bring life to those dimensions in the story. They are crucial to the story. Noteworthy is their character and their function in the overall story. Again character and function relate to one another.

When you choose your characters, you intentionally choose people who will have a function in your story.

But this doesn't help you to flesh out the character—what they look like and how they behave.

The Usefulness of Stereotypes

Stereotypes are an excellent starting point for character development. The paternal doctor, the anal accountant, the energetic senior citizen, the intellectual, the jock, the nerd, the princess, all of these stereotypes bring forward an instant snap-shot of a person.

At every age, across vocations, avocations, and cultures, stereotypes are instantly recognizable. That is the key to their usefulness.

In television and radio, rapid recognition is crucial. Consequently, stereotypes are very useful.

If you don't want to use a stereotype directly in your story, if you want to make that person seem fresher, twist the stereotype. Adding one characteristic or mixing stereotypes will give you a fresher character.

The intellectual jock, the pathological doctor, the prodigal senior citizen are all plays upon the original stereotype. But because they catch us by surprise, they also can effectively capture our interest, as well as create a character who is useful to your screen story.

There is an old expression that there is nothing new under the sun. Using stereotypes confirms and twisting stereotypes challenges this homily. Writers have to keep challenging homilies.

Dominant Characteristics

You've got a stereotype or you've decided to go against type. Now you have to give your character more flesh.

A very useful device is to give your character a dominant physical characteristic or behavioral characteristic. The secret with dominant characteristics is to make them purposeful. It's one thing to color your character; it's another to color them in a way that helps the plot.

Dominant physical characteristics should be extreme. The Georgio Armani detective ("Miami Vice"), the ethnic taxi driver ("Taxi"), the black cowboy ("Lonesome Dove"). Dominant behavioral characteristics should also be extreme. The dependent ex-wife ("Hill Street Blues"), the hysterical lawyer ("L.A. Law"), the father as ex-hippie ("Family Ties").

The principle of the dominant characteristic can be extended into a favorite phrase, a favorite attitude, or food or hobby. As we move through the narrative, the recurrence of this bit of information about the character, added to a dominant behavioral characteristic or physical characteristic, together gives us a stronger sense of the person.

The critical factor in making a dominant characteristic work for you is to have that characteristic relate to the premise of the story. The upshot is people who help rather than maintain a central position vis-à-vis your story.

The Active Character

What else is helpful in your main character is that he or she be active. It is very difficult to tell a story and to relate to the central character of the story when that character is passive.

Main characters engage with other characters when they are active. And they get into situations.

One Hollywood story editor describes the screen story as getting a character into trouble at the beginning of the story. As the character tries to get out of trouble, nature and the writer's plotting get him into even greater trouble. Considerable effort goes into getting out of trouble. Only an active character would act out energetically the effort to get out of trouble.

Passive characters, overly depressed characters, do not help screen stories. Indeed they pose real problems for your story.

The Active Character and the Urgent Plot

There is a relationship between the actor's willfulness and the story's sense of urgency or drive. The greater the character's effort and the greater the resistances he meets in the story, the greater the energy in the story.

This is the main reason it is best to think of the character and the story together. You can have a great plot but if the character isn't enmeshed as a person in it, your story loses its power.

We in the audience enter that story through the main character. Without empathy and identification for that main character, you, the writer, are in trouble.

MORE ON CHARACTERIZATION

You've got your character involved in the plot. And we're beginning to identify with your character. To deepen our involvement even further you can introduce the heroic factor.

Your Character as Hero

Audience's want to look up to main characters. Whether your main character is an ordinary person in extraordinary circumstances or an extraordinary person in ordinary circumstances, his behavior will invite us to view him at that moment in a heroic light.

Audiences want heroes; they know how few heroes they experience in real life. Part of their fantasy is that there are transcendent people and transcendent moments in life. It helps all of us cope with the realities that are more complex and not always so satisfying. Consequently, we in the audience virtually overidentify with the hero.

You can use this insight to develop your character and the situations you place him or her in. Pa Cartwright, Dr. Kildare, Ben Casey, Elliot Ness, all become heroes because of how they meet their life situations. Drama that recognizes this quality is very satisfying for an audience.

Charisma

You can help the issue of heroism if you also use characters who have some personal charisma.

Whether it is the charming arrogance of Alex in "Family Ties" or the intense commitment of Murphy Brown, we like certain types of people for good reason.

Charismatic people have intensity, conviction. They are not perfect but they are attractive. Often, they have the ability to laugh at themselves.

It is very difficult to identify with people who are the opposite—who have no beliefs, who are too perfect, or who take themselves so seriously that to laugh is a sign of personal weakness.

You can help your story if your main character has some charisma.

The Private Moment

All of us wear what I call a public face. We are social animals who most often keep our private thoughts and feelings to ourselves. So do characters in stories.

This posture keeps us distant from the characters. Good writers find opportunities to allow the audience private insights into their characters—that moment when the characters reveal themselves.

This is a very important moment for an audience. It is as if the character lets down his guard and lets us in. That instant may be painful or it may be joyful. The key element is that at that instant we see the real person and we feel privileged. The result is that we can identify in a broader way with your character.

The use of this type of moment of revelation can "cement" our relationship with your character. Good writers use this moment with all the characters in their story.

Main Characters and Secondary Characters

Now you have a sense of how to develop a character. You know that your main character should be active, empathic, and charismatic. What about your secondary characters?

Secondary characters are determined by function in the story. They can be there to advance the plot or they can be there for comic relief.

A useful way to divide secondary characters is to view them as either saints or sinners, with the main character trying to decide which he or she should be. Secondary characters line up on either side of the story premise or problem. They relate to the story as much as does the main character.

This doesn't help you tell us what they are like as people, although it points out a direction.

Secondary characters should be as interesting as main characters but they are more singular in their characteristics. Most of the time they are closer to a stereotype than the main character. A dominant physical or behavioral characteristic or both will help you develop those secondary characters.

A caution. Don't be afraid to make your secondary characters more interesting, more extreme, or more charismatic than your main character. Since your main character is conflicted, taken up by an issue, main characters often don't show as much emotion as secondary characters.

Think of it as the secondary character already committed, whereas your main character is still weighing options. Commitment is always more directly attractive or repellent, depending upon the goal of that commitment, than equivocation.

A special word about your most important secondary character, the antagonist of your story: in many ways, the antagonist represents the ultimate barrier to your main character. Consequently, the greater the antagonist, the more heroic the outcome will be perceived and the larger than life sense of your main character.

Antagonists aren't always supercriminals. Some of the most effective antagonists have been much closer. In the Cain and Abel Bible story, the protagonist and the antagonist are brothers. Fathers and sons, mothers and daughters, provide an opportunity for the writer to tell his or her story in stronger emotional terms than policeman–supercriminal.

The principal point about the antagonist is his or her relationship dramatically to your main character.

A final word. Use polarities whenever possible in presenting your characters. They should be different from one another. The more the differences in appearance and behavior, the more likely the small dramatic opportunities resulting will help you tell your story more effectively.

CHECKLIST

Before we turn to a practical example of character development in your story, a checklist is useful:

1. Is your character in the middle of your story?
2. Do your secondary characters line up on both sides of the story?
3. Have you used dominant physical/behavioral characteristics in developing your characters?
4. Do we like your main character?
5. Do we care about his or her fate?
6. Do we hate your antagonist?

DEVELOPING CHARACTERS: A PRACTICAL EXAMPLE

The story is as follows:

A dying father makes a confession to his 30-year-old daughter. He is not her father. He and his wife were childless. They kidnapped her as an infant. Now she herself is a mother. The father dies. And the daughter's world has been turned over. Who is she really? She must find out the answer.

Think of the story in three phases—her reaction to her father's confession, her search for her real parents, her reaction to what she finds.

There are naturally many dimensions that we could explore. How does her new family—her husband and her daughter (infant) relate to this deathbed confession and its result on the young woman? Is this going to be an urban-rural story or rural-rural, or rural-urban (the first designation describes where the young woman grew up; the second where she comes from and where she searches for her original parents). Do we want to complicate the story with cultural/racial dimensions? An example would be that the woman was originally Native American or half-breed or that she is now a Native American, but her family of origin was white. This latter type of decision will complicate the drama, a quality you may or may not want.

In terms of characters, the following are probable:

1. The young woman
2. Her husband
3. Her father (dying)
4. Her original father
5. Her original mother
6. Friends/professionals/acquaintances who help her or illuminate the nature of culture of origin
7. A love interest from her culture of origin
8. Siblings—old family/new family

Let's develop this cast of characters, keeping in mind the crucial question, do they help in the telling of this story?

The young woman is a mother and a wife. She would appear on the surface to be living a normal life. Dramatically, this revelation by her father should help explain certain clues in her life that, together, suggest that she is not whole. Consequently, in spite of being normal, it would be purposeful to give her qualities that suggest differences. This means that if she lives in a conservative community, she should be something of a rebel. If she lives in a commune, she should be the one striving for individualism.

Moving in closer, we can give her a dominant physical characteristic that differentiates her. If they are dark-complexioned, she should be fair. If they have exaggerated features, hers should be fine. In order to assure her membership in the community, she should share patterns of speech, education, hobbies with those prevailing in the community.

In terms of a dominant behavioral characteristic, she should exhibit differentness relative to her dying father and her husband. She might have an abiding interest in the past or in other cultures. If she is an archaeologist or a history teacher or an archivist, she would have a rational outlet for these interests. And her obsession with things past should separate her in a variety of ways from the present. When she does go to look for her past, she will be well prepared. Her predisposition to study the pasts of others will equip her better but also help us understand a key element to her personality—part of her always knew she didn't belong in the present she found herself in.

The young woman's husband is an opportunity for us to use someone who wants desperately to hold together the present. If his wife's past is a lie, it is possible that the rest of her current life—her marriage, her love for him—is also a lie.

It is not a good idea to make the husband a hysterical character. Rather, he should be a professional who has to mask his hysteria. An accountant or a professor, both are accustomed to communicating in an extremely civil manner. You can never tell what is going on underneath. But there are hints. This is a good approach to the husband. He is a man struggling to control himself, his environment, his wife, and so on. This need for control could be his dominant behavioral characteristic.

In terms of a dominant physical characteristic, a good shading would be in response to his dominant behavioral characteristic. When we visualize a person who needs so much control, we conjure up an insecure individual. What if the husband was the best looking man in town, the man all the women chased after. He appears to be the opposite of the insecure individual his behavior suggests. In this way , the good-looking, controlling man presents a man who isn't what he appears to be. This begins to upset the stereotype and the unexpected side can help us dramatically.

Turning to the dying father, we need less characterization but what we do get is important. What we need here is surprise. That surprise should relate to the confession. Don't forget he is confessing to kidnapping, a crime so serious that in the past the punishment was as severe as for murder. He should not look like a kidnapper. A good surprise is that he is the minister in the town. The idea of a minister kidnapping a child makes the crime more heinous and the dramatic elements of the scene more heightened. The key choice is to make him a person as far from a kidnapper as possible—the town doctor, the mayor, and so on.

He should be a benevolent father or the confession will be undermined.

What about the original father? What should he be like? Should he be similar or different from the dead father? Does he have other children? Did he ever get over the kidnapping?

Here it is best to upset our expectations. In our minds we hope a parent never gets over this sort of trauma. If so, what if he has gotten over the kidnapping and lived a full and satisfying life (just as the dead father lived a life carrying an unbearable secret). Try to make him different from the dead father. This means different in his station in life and in his attitude. This will allow maximum latitude for the daughter to have to relate to. He has to be a totally new challenge to her expectations.

As to the mother, you have a choice. She should be the one who never got over the kidnapping. Your choice is whether she is a functioning, soulful casualty or whether she is the dysfunctional, hidden-away casualty. It depends upon how much of a role you want her to play in the story. It could be useful if the mother-daughter reunion has a meaning distinct from the reunion with the father. The mother could offer our main character a connectedness with the past (which she has never left) and dramatic opportunities for healing.

Acquaintances/friends or professionals should play a very subsidiary role in the story, since the family(s) should remain the central focus of the drama. If we use these characters they should be quickly drawn and relate to the story. A friend who always plays the lost soul would be useful. So too an adopted person who has always lived in two worlds. If we use a social worker we might make the social worker an adopted person, thereby blending two dramatic functions into the same person. The usefulness here is to condense the drama so that the intensity isn't diluted. Too many characters water down the dramatic soup!

If we want to complicate the story more, we can introduce a love interest for the young woman, but that person would have to come on the scene in the search for her family of origin. Such a person should be developed in the context of the husband. He should also have something to do with the life of her parents of origin.

We can also complicate this story by introducing siblings in either sphere—the present or from the past. Those siblings can be very useful to illustrate what the young woman never had. The story can also be complicated if her sibling in her family of origin is a twin.

In this practical example, the key elements are the relationship of character to function. What I hope I have also suggested is that when you develop characters, you try to surprise us. And as a writer, that you always be on the lookout for dramatic opportunities.

Now let's turn to what your characters will say.

5

Your Characters Talk

In radio, dialogue is everything. In television, it is important but the visual component offers options not available in radio.

Dialogue serves specific purposes. Dialogue can be used to characterize or it can be used to advance the plot. Or it can be used for comic relief.

In both mediums, you are trying to entertain as well as to inform the audience. Varying the techniques at your disposal will help entertain and inform that audience. The implication is to not depend on dialogue to accomplish everything, where possible.

Where you have to use dialogue, you don't have to be intimidated. You can use simple, direct dialogue. But that dialogue should relate to function. I'll get back to function a little later. Before I do, it is best to suggest ways to cut down on what the dialogue has to accomplish for you.

SETTING UP THE ACTION

You want to avoid a dialogue situation where no more than two people are sitting talking to one another—it takes the form of a question and answer session. The result is tedious for the viewer and listener because nothing else is happening. If the two people were involved in action, the dialogue would arise out of their reaction to their situation.

In fact, the dialogue can be responses to a variety of qualities in the scene. The dialogue can be:

1. a response to the situation
2. a reaction to each other
3. comic relief
4. reference to the plotting
5. reference to characterization
6. a connective statement leading into the next scene

The dialogue, because of ongoing action, is masked because we, the audience, are involved in the evolving action of the scene. Where we are simply watching a two person dialogue with no background action, we quickly grow aware of the artificiality of the dialogue.

ENERGIZING DIALOGUE

Reflective statements, overuse of passive tenses, and neutral words will sap the energy out of dialogue.

If you use active tenses your dialogue will read like it is evolving right now. If you use short phrases rather than full sentences or paragraphs, it will appear as if your dialogue is evolving quickly right now. You can also help pace if you cut out unnecessary words.

A good example is the piece of narration that begins "There was a time. . ." What time? Are you referring to yesteryear, the past, or to the recent past? Be specific. Is there a single word that says what you were using an entire clause for? Is so, use it. If it is a comparison use "Then. . ." and "Now. . ." If it is a statement, use "the Past . . ."

Another example is the "If only. . ." conditional statement. This is too tentative for dialogue. If you want to suggest a character's hesitation or ambivalence use "maybe."

What about neutral words as opposed to emotional words? The following examples will give you a sense of the difference.

NEUTRAL	EMOTIONAL
travel	run, drive, fly
reconcile	hug
equivalent	the same
obese	heavy
ill	sick
humor	laughs
mature	grow up
bookish	nerd

Emotional words tend to be active words that are widely used in nonprofessional conversation. They can be colloquial slang and tend to give feeling to the speaker's association or real meaning.

You are best off when characters feel strongly in their scenes. This means emotion-laden language. The shorter the phrases, the less your characters speak in sentences, the more emotional the dialogue.

MAKING DIALOGUE BELIEVABLE

Besides being energetic, dialogue should be believable.

Here, specificity again is the key.

People come from somewhere. Dialogue is specific to a location, a time, a profession. Particular phrases, words, and colloquialisms signify particular places or professions. A writer can be creative but you can't write what you don't know. If your story takes place in a particular region of the country, that local pattern of speech and colloquialisms will have to make its way into the dialogue.

To pick up that pattern, you will have to speak to people from that region or travel with your tape recorder to capture examples of that speech on your recorder. If you are writing a story about urban lawyers and you yourself are not a lawyer, you should tape record their dialogue whether it be in the office or the courtroom.

Beyond the surface place or profession pattern of speech, there is the other facet to a character's speech—the nature of their emotional make-up and how that affects their language. Your character can be an astrophysicist from Corpus Cristi but if he or she is in emotional crisis, the emotional component of the instant will dominate their dialogue.

The character's background and emotional state will make the general pattern of language believable. But more technical adjustments are necessary to make the dialogue seem believable.

If the situation is a friendly conversation, the dialogue will have to seem spontaneous or stiff—depending on the state of the characters. If the situation is a lecture, the language will have to be formal and elaborate, in keeping with what we expect from a lecture. At all times the specific situation will dictate another set of parameters for the dialogue.

Believability results when dialogue seems true to both the situation and the nature of the characters. Because believability can be elusive, the more specific you are about who the people are and their emotional state at that time, the more likely the audience will believe that they are listening to real people saying real things.

A caution. Viewers and listeners today are media-wise. They've listened to a lot of dialogue. And they know movie and TV dialogue very well. There is a tendency in writers to mimic that dialogue pattern, mainly because as dialogue it seems vivid.

There are the famous lines from *Marty*:

"What do you want to do Saturday night, Angie?"
"I don't know, Marty. What do you want to do?"

or the "hold the mayonnaise" dialogue sequence from *Five Easy Pieces*. In both cases the dialogue is flashy, it draws a lot of attention to itself. Perhaps this is why young writers like to ape the pattern.

My advice is to avoid it when you are conscious that you're falling into mimicry. The problem with using movie dialogue is that it can be so mannered that it takes us away from the emotions of the scene and makes the characters less credible. We know we are watching a TV movie rather than relating to the characters as if they were real people.

By using movie dialogue the writer is drawing attention to himself or herself and suggesting his or her own cleverness rather than allowing for the audience to relate directly with the characters. The temptation is there; it is a lot easier than writing dialogue that arises out of the emotions of the scene. We all like to be clever. But this is one area where the writer should resist the impulse.

MAKING DIALOGUE DRAMATIC

You begin to make dialogue dramatic when the dialogue is a reaction to the situation. You also help when the words you use are emotion-laden.

But the key to dramatic dialogue is to set up polarities. The goals of the characters in a scene should be opposite to one another. This is one set of polarities. The nature of the characters, their dominant characteristics, should present another set of polarities. The more opposites that operate in a scene, the better for the dramatic quality of your dialogue.

The dialogue, in order to be dramatic, should also follow the dramatic pattern of the scene. For example, the emotional character of the usual scene starts low and rises to an apex (where the point of the scene is presented) and then falls to the end of the scene. To simulate this pattern, the dialogue at that apex should be shorter and more emotional than before or after. And the words you use at that point should be different than at any other point in the scene.

A brief example will illustrate dramatic dialogue.

Two male students are about to write an exam. They are concerned. But one of them is more concerned about the other's advances on his girlfriend.

>   CARL
> Another ten minutes.

>   SAM
> What about the two hour exam?

>   CARL
> It's the next ten minutes that are rough.

>   SAM
> If you know biology...

>   CARL
> Birds and bees...

>   SAM
> Boys and girls...

>   CARL
> Speaking of girls, I saw Susan on my way in.

>   SAM
> I hope she's praying for me.

>   CARL
> I asked her out.

>   SAM
> What?!

>   CARL
> It was a test.

>   SAM
> I'm your best friend.

>   CARL
> She's not for you.

> SAM
>
> I'm going crazy.

> CARL
>
> Relax. I've taken a burden off your hands. Now you can concen-
> trate on the exam.

> SAM
>
> You think you know everything.

> CARL
>
> It was a test. She didn't have to say yes. But she said yes.
> Now you know. She's not for you.

> SAM
>
> Thanks. Buddy.

Notice that Sam's dialogue becomes briefer, more intense, once Carl tells him he's asked Susan out. At the apex Sam uses words such as "best" and "crazy." His dialogue is also more brief than Carl's. In fact, Carl's dialogue is relatively lengthy. Notice also that they are very different in their attitude towards the exam and their goals are in opposition to one another around the issue of Susan. Here polarities are working to help the dramatic quality of the scene.

A final point. The dramatic focus of the scene is Carl's invitation to Susan and Sam's response, in essence, Carl's attempt to steal Sam's girlfriend. The examination is the background of the scene.

Repetition in dialogue emphasizes the dramatic point.

Carl's line: "It was a test. She didn't have to say yes. But she said yes. Now you know. She's not for you."

Each part of this line "a test," "said yes" and "she's not for you" is repeated here from elsewhere in the scene. Repetition emphasizes a point being made in the dialogue. It says to the audience, what you are hearing is important, dramatically important.

Repetition is also used in dialogue to underscore dramatic importance.

MAKING DIALOGUE CONTINUOUS

Another problem facing the writer is how to make the dialogue flow in a continuous manner.

In part, continuity can be gained technically through repetition strategically presented.

For example, if the last word spoken by one character is repeated first by the other character, the illusion of continuity is affirmed.

> CHARACTER 1
>
> We are leaving in the morning for Iowa city.

> CHARACTER 2
>
> Iowa city! What are we going to do in Iowa city?

```
               CHARACTER 1
     Iowa city is quiet.

               CHARACTER 2
     Quiet is good for babies. Adults need noise.
```

In these four lines of dialogue the pattern of continuity is highlighted by the repetition of "Iowa city" and "quiet."

The principle of hooking dialogue lines one to another operates to link scenes to one another. In this case, the repetition at the end of the first scene is repeated at the beginning of the next. The repetition can be a word, a phrase, or a similar speech pattern. Each can accomplish the goal—to make one scene link with the next.

Continuity can also be established by the linkage of a phrase with a particular character. When the phrase recurs it brings particular implications but most important it provides a sense of continuity. Perhaps the most remembered piece of dialogue of this sort is Dirty Harry Callahan's "Make my day." Writers very often like to give their characters distinct dialogue "bites." It makes the character distinct but more important, it helps the problem of dialogue continuity.

Finally, dialogue continuity is established by creating a pattern of speech for each character. As that pattern recurs, we recognize the person by the pattern and his or her presence later with expectations of continuity. When we know the character, we experience the character's dialogue as continuous. Unless the writer veers from the character, we will stay with the expectation of continuity.

DIALOGUE AND FUNCTION

As we have discussed, characters in a story serve a purpose. For the main character, his or her purpose is to make a choice. For the secondary characters, they are present to advance the plot or for comic relief.

Dialogue, in terms of pure content, should relate to function. If the character is in the story to get the main character from Point A to Point B, that character's dialogue is about:

1. Point A
2. The roadblocks to Point B
3. Point B

The two characters may fall in love between Point A and Point B, in which case we could add to the dialogue:

4. Their past
5. Their hopes for the future
6. Other lovers

But what is excluded from that secondary character's dialogue is anything that doesn't help the relationship or their making their way to Point B.

Your test for dialogue is "does it help the story?" or more loosely, "does it have any relationship with the story?"

You are on safe ground when dialogue relates character to function in the story. Needless to say, if you don't know a character's purpose in a story, you are likely to get into dialogue trouble.

DIRECT DIALOGUE VS. INDIRECT

The implication of my comments about character and function suggests that a main character's dialogue would reflect that character's indecision about making a choice. But this is not the case. Here, the writer has to make the directness. Writers mask intentions by using indirect language. The characters react to the situation, but they are not entirely aware of the solution, at least not until the last act of the story.

Consequently, indirectness can suggest confusion, anguish, avoidance. A practical example will help make the point.

A character is contemplating a change in career. She has been given poor advice by a career counsellor. She is unsure whether she can trust people's opinions. All she knows is she must pursue another career. The following conversation takes place between the woman, Judy, and her husband, Alan.

ALAN

```
Selling condos is too easy. You could sell in the night and
play all day.
```

JUDY

```
This is a serious problem and you make jokes as bad as that
career counsellor.
```

ALAN

```
Lighten up. You won't get the right job until you can lighten
up.
```

JUDY

```
I'm not making enough to hire a gag writer.
```

ALAN

```
I'll sell you a few jokes.
```

JUDY

```
Maybe I'll go back to school.
```

ALAN

```
And what would you study?
```

JUDY

```
Business maybe? I could get a Master's.
```

ALAN

```
You've learned enough.
```

                              JUDY
And I know nothing.

                              ALAN
You know how to sell condos.

                              JUDY
And you don't know how to do anything else.

                              ALAN
But I'm the happy one.

                              JUDY
Maybe. Maybe not.

In this scene, Judy is tense about not liking her job. When her husband makes suggestions she doesn't directly talk about her unhappiness or her problem with the career counsellor. Instead she is indirect—she talks about school, she attacks her husband. This indirect dialogue alludes to her unhappiness and alerts us to her indecision and to the fact that there is a problem. She doesn't have to be direct about her problem. In fact the dialogue is more tense if she is indirect.

DIALOGUE AND HUMOR

Often dialogue is used to siphon off the tension in a scene. Dialogue that is witty or amusing is often present to release tension in the scene.

Usually this dialogue is associated with a particular character whose function in the story is to provide comic relief.

Humorous dialogue is not a character telling a joke. The dialogue has to arise out of a dramatic situation.

Two dialogue responses to a particular dramatic situation will illustrate the point.

A sailor is stuck in a lifeboat with his captain. They are the only two survivors of a shipwreck.

A serious interchange about rescue would go as follows:

                              SAILOR
We have food for two days.

                              CAPTAIN
If they caught the SOS, the Coast Guard will find us before we
drift too far east.

                              SAILOR
I wish the flares weren't lost.

                              CAPTAIN
Save your concern. You'll need the energy.

A humorous version of this scene would go accordingly:

```
                          SAILOR
      We have food, but no caviar, sir.

                          CAPTAIN
      The last SOS was for caviar. If we drift far enough east we can
      catch our own.

                          SAILOR
      No flares left to frighten the salmon.

                          CAPTAIN
      Then you'll have to use your imagination.
```

The situation hasn't changed. But the sailor and the captain respond to that situation differently in the humorous version than they do in the other.

Humor can be very useful to underscore the problems facing the two characters in the situation. In one sense it alleviates the tension. In another it suggests to the audience that these two people intend to survive.

HEIGHTENED DIALOGUE VS. NATURAL DIALOGUE

A writer should recognize the relationship between language and medium.

In the theater, heightened language is in order. Heightened language is the equivalent of high octane dialogue. It can be poetic, philosophical, charged. Generally it is a reflection of the intensity of the character but in the theater it is also the expression of the playwright. Heightened dialogue is purposeful relating to character and plot advancement but it is also editorial, presenting the viewpoint of the playwright.

Heightened language is appropriate for radio but it is not appropriate for television.

Television is for the most part a naturalistic medium; it looks real. Consequently naturalistic dialogue is appropriate for television. Indeed, the more TV dialogue sounds real, the more likely TV characters will look and sound real to the audience. It is critical for the television writer to use naturalistic dialogue. This means colloquialisms, it means regional speech, and it means the avoidance of florid speech.

Now that your characters can speak, let's turn to writing specific genres; our first, the radio documentary.

6

Writing a Radio Documentary

You know where to find ideas and how to develop them for impact. Good ideas presented with dramatic values will present well in both radio and television.

But for radio more specific requirements must be met, particularly an emphasis on the verbal—interviews and narration. But what else is required is a sense of immediacy in the manner of presentation.

WHAT TYPE OF DOCUMENTARY

There are numerous types of documentaries. They fall into three general categories—public affairs, advocacy, and personal portrait.

The public affairs documentary embraces current political and social issues as well as past or historical perspectives particularly as they relate to ongoing developing issues of importance. Advocacy documentaries deal with public affairs issues but from a distinct point of view. They are trying to make a case to prove that their point of view should prevail over the status quo. The personal portrait is a documentary form that focuses on a personality or on a community.

At one level all of these documentaries have an educational component. They are trying to inform the audience about their subject. The point of view they take may vary from reflective/historical to subjective or highly personal. Different types of documentary lend themselves to particular treatments. The personal portrayal for example lends itself to a subjective treatment, while the public affairs documentary generally requires a more reflective treatment.

GOOD SUBJECTS

The daily newspaper tells us the issues of the day, what the public is concerned with. Good radio documentaries have a relationship with those ideas/issues.

For example, if social security pensioners divide into have and have nots and this reality is news, we have potentially a social issue story with a personal dimension. A personal interest approach might be a portrait of a senior citizen couple who use their social security monies to set up a food bank to feed needy senior citizens. This approach combines an important issue of the day with a personal angle.

Similarly, in the realm of public affairs, a documentary on the closing of a U.S. steel plant in Pittsburgh might give the writer and the producer the opportunity to either portray Steeltown (Pittsburgh) or the rise and fall of the steel industry.

This type of documentary will always be influenced by the production unit. If it is local radio (i.e., local Pittsburgh) the focus would emphasize the local dimensions of the history, the community, the workers, the managers, and then the influence on the growth of the city. If the documentary was commissioned for national broadcast, a more national perspective would be the most important, i.e., the steel industry in the context of American industry; even in the context of the German and Japanese steel industries.

The critical factor determining the content will be the audience for whom the documentary is intended.

WHO IS YOUR AUDIENCE?

As mentioned earlier in the book, to know the audience you write for may be the single most important factor in determining how the show will be written.

If your audience is 18-25 years old, the nature of the material and how it is presented will differ considerably from the approach you take for a female, over-40 audience. To present your material, you need to know the answer to this question.

It isn't good enough to say "I want to reach as many people as possible."

Once you have determined your audience, you can decide upon the balance of information to entertainment values in the script. To a certain extent all radio documentaries need a degree of entertainment value, but if the audience is principally primed or interested, you don't have to be quite as entertaining. But you do have to give them the amount of information they are looking for. An example will illustrate the challenge.

The program you are writing is about natural childbirth methods. The primary audience for the program is women but the program is targeted mainly for expectant mothers and fathers. This audience is highly motivated to listen and what they want (aside from reassurance) is information.

If the program were to be geared for teenagers, for example, it would have to be broadened into a script about the next phase, marriage and children. And to reach that audience it would have to be much more focused on entertainment values.

Another way of looking at this issue of audience is to look at the trade-off of information and emotion in your script. All scripts should have an emotional dimension to them. To reach all audiences, the emotional quality plays a crucial role.

Emotion, information, entertainment values will help you reach your audience. To use these tools most effectively you must know, first and foremost, who your audience is.

HOW TO START

Your assignment is a 30-minute documentary on childbirth. You've never had a child, you know little about the subject. What do you do?

The goal is to make yourself an expert as quickly as you can. You don't have much time. The producer has an air date in two weeks.

To gather the proper information you should begin with the experts. Call childbirth education experts, associations, pediatricians of particular differing methods. And of course you should talk to people who have recently had children by this method as well as some who have not.

Talking to these people on the phone will give you potential other sources. From your lists you will eventually have to decide who to interview. Make sure you talk to a cross section of experts in the field. You should supplement your research with books, articles, and newspaper stories on the subject.

Tape recorder in hand, you will be able to tape interviews.

Having gathered a great deal of information, the shaping of your radio documentary begins.

STRUCTURING THE RADIO DOCUMENTARY

Having completed your research and knowing the audience for your story, you can begin to give the documentary a point of view.

Because radio is an audio medium, language will organize the information. The most important interpretive tool for us, the listeners, is a point of view.

Once you have presented your point of view in the documentary, we, the listeners, have the filter through which all the information can be interpreted.

THE CENTRALITY OF POINT OF VIEW

Think of your radio documentary as a series of sequences. The first sequence presents the issue, time, place, and the point of view. The sequences that follow elaborate on the dimensions of the story. But the shaping and selection of material within those sequences is organized to affirm or relate to that original point of view presented in the first sequence.

To return to our example, the 30 minute documentary on childbirth, let's assume that the point of view taken is that the new methods of childbirthing, particularly the natural methods, are best for the child.

The sequence then, will tell us about the new methods as well as the old with the focus on the benefits for the child. Some sequences will focus on the risks to the mother, the medical stance, the historical evolution of birthing procedures. In each sequence references should be made to the benefits or risks to the child (since what is best for the child is central to the point of view).

Given our point of view, we are in effect making a case supporting natural childbirth as a healthier option for the newborn.

The benefit of the point of view is that it not only helps shape the selection of material, it also directs the audience toward a conclusion; that natural childbirth methods are best for the newborn. Point of view gives your documentary dramatic direction.

THE SEQUENCE

The sequence approach is a useful way to fragment your documentary; it's easier to work with. And you will be able to check if each sequence is doing something different from the others. In order to make sequences relate to one another, however, it's not enough that each expresses a similar point of view.

Each sequence can have similar detail patterns. For example, interviews with the same individuals will recur in different sequences. Perhaps an individual will present the expert opinion, another the point of view, and another the more emotional dimensions of the documentary.

When these patterns recur over various sequences, the sense of continuity is reinforced.

Another dimension of the sequence is that there be present an informational dimension as well as an emotional dimension. Particular voices should be associated with each. This balance also forms part of a pattern that suggests continuity in the documentary.

Finally, a narrator will lend the sense of continuity, editorial view, and the linkage between sequences. Since narration is so important in the radio documentary we will talk about it more comprehensively later in this chapter.

RISING ACTION

The sequences in your documentary should be organized on the principle of rising action. That is to say after your explanatory opening sequence, your most powerful sequence should be the last. That sequence should restate the point of view but, more importantly, it should represent the dramatic climax.

The idea of rising action implies your developing a sense of which sequence has the greatest impact. But it also implies that you develop a sense of where the documentary is going and how each sequence can work to get it closer to that climax.

Writing a documentary is a bit like sorting out a puzzle. We know what it will look like at the end. And we know that we are more and more excited as we see the end in sight.

The writing process however has less guesswork and you have to be deliberate in organizing the sequences.

One other factor will affect how you organize the sequences. You will have to choose a mix of information and emotion. It may be that the sequences have both qualities. Or there may be sequences that are in turn emotional, the next informational. Only you can decide what will suit the idea best. As stated earlier, knowing who your audience is will help you in this choice.

To restate the critical point here, organize your sequences along a line of rising action. Your last sequence should be the strongest.

EMOTION

No matter how dry your subject, it is critical to employ tactics to generate an emotional dimension to your documentary. Audiences remember how they feel about other people. No matter how large scale the event, it is the personal dimension that touches us.

Consequently, you can't tell your story exclusively in terms of statistics and expert opinions.

As I mentioned earlier, the degree of emotional qualities depends upon the nature of your audience.

How to generate that emotional response is varied. Of course the personal observation of a key participant; the mother in our natural childbirth story, for example. But this is only one way.

Conflict within your story, opposing opinions, a situation that didn't work out as expected, these types of situations will generate emotions.

But probably nothing will be as effective as "actuality" sequences. In the case of the natural childbirth documentary, this would be the sounds of the birthing process with all it unpredictability, excitement, and anticipation. The inclusion of this sort of "live" material is more valuable and emotional than any number of interviews.

The critical point here is that your documentary should have an emotional component.

INFORMATION

How much information is enough? This is a question you will have to answer.

The key operational consideration here is credibility. You need enough hard information in your documentary so that you have established the credibility of the show.

In most instances this means a great deal of information. Often, even if the audience is informed on the subject, some background information as well as contemporary views on the subject are necessary.

Most often that information should come in the early phases of the documentary.

The information you include can be statistical, biographical, or expert. Regional, national, and international observations lend perspective to that information.

The delivery of the information can be via interview or the narrator.

Wherever possible information can be "humanized" when it takes an anecdotal form. For example, in our natural childbirth documentary, in the sequence describing past practices, a letter from a new parent describing the procedure to her father circa 1790 would be a vivid way to convey the sense of practices of that time.

Wherever possible anecdotal or even humorous observation will make information less dry and consequently, your documentary will be more vivid.

TENSION

Too often writers associate the term documentary with literal realism. This slice of life definition too often implies a lack of dramatic values (since dramatic values imply manipulation of reality rather than its presentation).

This circular set of assumptions has ruined many a documentary!

Dramatic values—conflict, polarities, protagonists and antagonists—are no less necessary in the documentary.

Attention to dramatic values in your documentary will help generate the tension you need to hold on to the listener.

In the radio documentary you want the listener to understand the flow of ideas but you also want that listener to care about the issue and finally to relate to your point of view.

This can only happen by the deployment of tension and conflict throughout the documentary.

In our natural childbirth documentary, this can happen through the presentation of opposing views. It can also be presented through the presentation of an empathic person whose experiences we follow (will it work out well?). Tension also generates from anecdotal historical material. For example, the abandonment of female new-borns in specific ancient cultures, cultures where natural childbirth was practiced by the mother going away from the community, giving birth on her own, and then finally having to give up the child because it was female. This point refers directly back to the central issue of the show—that natural childbirth is, in principle, good for the child. Our example suggests that in the historical instances cited, it wasn't good for the child if the child was female!

The general modulation of tension throughout the documentary will come primarily from the interplay of the emotional and the informational dimensions of the material. Beyond this continuing clash, the deployment of dramatic values where possible will enhance the tension and the consequent sense of involvement in the documentary.

CONTINUITY

The issues of continuity are particular within sequences but also are important in the linking of each sequence to another.

Perhaps the best way to concretize the way to provide continuity is to list the *methods*:

1. A clear statement of the purpose or point of view or goal of the documentary in the first sequence. As long as the sequences that follow adhere to that point of view, general continuity will be present.
2. A logical progression through sequences. This might be a chronological progression or it might proceed on the basis of "making a case." In either case the pattern should be clear and adhered to.

3. The presence of a line of information sources that reappear fulfilling similar functions throughout the sequences. This might be an expert being interviewed.
4. A consistency across sequences in the sources of emotion. Particular people being interviewed throughout the sequences can fulfill this purpose as well.
5. The narrator will give you the continuity you haven't achieved in all of the above patterns.

So far what I've mentioned gives you a general pattern of continuity. What about the specific?

As in our discussion of dialogue, specific continuity can come from a speech pattern of one person to the speech pattern or regional dialect of another. Or it can come from the simple repetition of a phrase by one speaker being echoed by another.

Specific continuity from one sequence to another will come from the narrator whose voice carries over from one sequence to another. He simply changes the idea he is dealing with and at that instant we are in the next sequence.

The role of the narrator is so important that we should spend the next section on the role of the narrator in radio documentary.

NARRATION

Called commentary in the United Kingdom, narration is a central feature of your radio documentary.

I've already suggested its role in continuity but the importance of the narration is much more far-reaching.

The tone of the narrator can lend authority, emotion, a point of view to the actual narration. The tone can be whatever the material requires.

By tone I'm not referring to the choice of performer to read the narration, but rather to the choice of words and their organization. If they are neutral, the tone is authoritative. If the words are active, opinionated, the tone is passionate. If the words are colloquial, the tone is warm and so on.

Your choice of words in narration is a crucial decision.

Your next decision is how much narration. Here, less is more. Try to write spare. Too many words require time and more concentration to take in. Simpler phrasing gives us time to absorb the ideas.

Don't write narration as if you were writing a speech. Try to relate it to the ideas central to the sequence. And then present those ideas in as simplified, linguistically, a manner as possible.

There are times that you may want to elaborate or comment on what has been said in an interview. Again, do so in the narration but get right to the point. Often you will find the narration is important to explain a point made in the interview.

If too much information has been stated in the interview, you may have to simplify or present an idea that will help us absorb the information quickly. In a situation like this it is usually the sharpened comment of the narrator that pulls the interview together or highlights the point of the interview.

To summarize the role of the narrator it is crucial that each of these dimensions be present in the narration:

1. Continuity between sequences
2. Presentation and reiteration of the point of view
3. Editorial comment on the interviews
4. Explanation of the central point of the interview material
5. Reiteration of critical points made in interviews
6. To present a tone that underscores the emotions of sequences
7. To elaborate upon informational sequences

Narration writing is a skill but if you are going to write a radio documentary you must try it and try to master narration writing. It is a central feature of the radio documentary.

FORMAT

The proper format for radio documentary can vary but essentially it falls into one of three accepted categories.

```
1.  Name:              Dialogue:
     (name of speaker)      (interview or narration)


2.  Name:            Sound Effects:        Dialogue:


3.  Narration:                     Interview:
     Name:                         Name:
```

The first includes narration and effects directly into the ordering of the sequence. An example of the first will provide you with a sample format.

```
            NATURAL CHILDBIRTH 1990
              a radio documentary
            by _____
            for _____ Radio
            producer _____

               contact:     Your Name
                            Address
                            Telephone
```

```
Sequence I
1.  Sundry voices in a delivery room.
     NURSE            Gently, now push gently.
     DOCTOR           You're doing very well, Mrs. Foster.
     MRS. FOSTER      It's coming out! It's coming!
2.  SOUND EFFECT  MRS. FOSTER CRIES OUT.
3.  SOUND DISSOLVE  A BABY'S FIRST CRY.
```

4.	NURSE	You've got a beautiful baby.
5.	DOCTOR	It's a girl. Congratulations.
6.	NARRATOR	Jenny Foster has a daughter. She's on top of the world. She had her baby without anesthetic. She wanted, as many women today do, to have her child naturally. What does this fascination mean? Is it a fad? Jenny Foster didn't think so.
		We're going to look at this issue of natural childbirth in the next half hour. We'll talk to experts, to the historians, to the advocates and to the oppositionAnd, of course, we'll talk to Jenny Foster.

END OF SEQUENCE I.

This brief sample format gives you a sense of how the radio documentary is presented. Narration plays a role. So do personalities and so does action, in this case a birth.

Note how in this sequence the goal and the parameters of the show are introduced.

It is critical for you to present your material in the proper format.

When in doubt, ask the producer for a sample script from their program. As you will learn there can be slight variations between producers. But in essence, the example here presented will give you a good base for your format.

One last word. Some producers want music excerpts included. You can make reference if you incorporate music, right in the body, just as sound effects were described. Many producers however prefer to select their own music and will probably ignore your suggestions.

Now, on to radio drama.

7

▼ Writing a Radio Drama
▼
▼
▼
▼

The radio drama is a particular form that is currently making a comeback. Before television, this form provided the sitcoms, the soaps, and the miniseries of their day.

Today's radio drama performs a different function. Linked to the theater and literature, radio drama differs in its source material from radio drama of the pre-television period.

This doesn't mean radio drama has to be stuffy! Witness Doug Adam's "The Hitchhiker's Guide to the Galaxy." The radio drama series was so innovative and exciting it was broadcast all over the world. Indeed it is still broadcast and read. A series of books has followed the original series. And a series of audio tapes are now for sale. Just as people are buying video copies of the old "I Love Lucy" shows, they are also buying copies of the radio series.

In order to begin a detailed look at how to write a radio drama, it is useful to begin with the differences and similarities to the radio documentary.

Like the documentary, radio drama depends upon language and upon a flow of ideas that have to be simplified for continuity and then amplified for credibility. Sound effects, music, and dialogue are the only tools the writer of both forms has at his disposal.

And like the radio documentary, radio drama can choose as its subject matter, day-to-day issues and an approach that is essentially realistic. Radio documentary, most often, does approach material along these realistic parameters.

But radio drama can also be presented using an approach that is far from real-ism. When the drama concentrates upon the tension between the inner life of a char-acter and his or her outer actions, the radio drama embraces a broad range of options. And when this tension is treated with imagination, the writer can begin to imply what the listener cannot see. It may be psychological terror. It may be ecstatic love. It can be anything. And here is the strength of radio drama. Its appeal must be to the richness of the listener's imagination, to those inner recesses rarely, if ever, shown on the more literal, visual medium, television.

That is not to say that the radio drama writer can sidestep issues of who is your audience or the use of dramatic values in his or her story. The writer cannot! But the radio drama writer must recognize that the inner life of characters is the bread and butter of the radio drama.

INNER LIFE

A man sits at a desk and writes a letter. What is he thinking and feeling at that instant? He may be dreaming about a childhood incident. He may be reviling an associate. He may be consumed by desire for the woman next door, a person he's been unable to speak to for the past 10 years.

Whether it is fear or fantasy, what we see is a man at a desk writing a letter. At least that's all that we would see if this scene was presented in an audiovisual medium like television. On the radio, however, we can explore any of the above-mentioned thoughts, fixations, or fantasies. These elements make up the character's inner life. And through an inner monologue the character can tell us what he is thinking about while writing the letter. Radio drama thrives when it dramatizes the inner life of its characters.

INNER CONFLICT

Just as inner life can be rich in thoughts and fantasies, it is also rich in inner conflict.

Writers need only look at Freud's ideas about the unconscious to come up against a ready-made theory of conflict.

Freud's theories about drives and inhibitions can be simplified to his theories' dimensions of unconscious life—the id, that part of the unconscious that is made up of drives—hunger, aggression, sexuality. The id functions in the context of two other dimensions—the superego or conscience and the ego, a mediating force that functions to bring equilibrium to bear between the id and the superego.

The id, the ego, and the superego provide a dynamic view of the unconscious; they also suggest in their constant interaction a world of constant inner conflict.

When joined to the lives of others, with their own inner lives and conflicts, one can imagine a community or a society either in constant conflict or involved in the effort to seek out ways to keep conflict in check. (Isn't that what real life is like!)

EXTERNAL CONFLICT

Relationships, partnerships, political campaigns, and wars represent levels of conflict from the interpersonal to the international. All levels of external conflict provide the radio drama writer potential for stories.

The focus of conflict should always be the individual character. How does the character feel inside about the external conflict? This depends upon the character's past but more important for radio drama, it depends upon the nature of the character's inner life.

In fact, the richness of radio drama is the ability to move us into the character's inner life, all while that character is dealing with an external conflict.

THE PRECIPITATING EVENT

A man aged 34 has never left home. He has few friends. And he preoccupies himself with a world of fantasy. His parents who have protected him all his life decide to go away for a holiday. They have never been apart. What happens to the young man is the substance of a half-hour radio drama.

In this story the precipitating event is the parent's decision to take a needed holiday, alone.

It is critical for the drama that the precipitating event be critical (and threatening) to the inner life of the character. Whether the precipitating event is a prescription for tragedy or an opportunity to change is the substance of this particular drama.

The precipitating event provides the writer with the "kickoff" to the drama.

But we need much more to make the drama work.

THE PRIVATE EAR

The critical path into the inner life is to create what I will call "the private ear." As the writer you want to give the listener a private pipeline to the thoughts of the main character.

The best vehicle for this is the inner monologue. And the inner monologue should contradict the superficial impression the listener has. Inside, everyone feels they are free, fascinating, and funny. This private side to the shy, retiring 34-year-old is the key to engaging us with his life. And it is the part of the character that the listener will relate to; because underneath we all feel like a blend of Don Juan and Woody Allen. This access to the inner life of the character is the benefit of the private ear.

As a writer, you have to feel free to access the inner life of your characters. If you don't, you'll keep us at arms length from them and your story will be less successful.

If, however, you do allow yourself to enter their inner lives, you will free your own instinctual sense of the dramatic possibilities and the result will be energetic and engaging.

STRUCTURE

Now you have access to the private responses of the character; and you have established a precipitating event which prompts an internal conflict for the character.

In order to flesh out the radio drama you have to decide upon the end point of the drama. If the story is narrative, there will be a logical narrative end; when the mission is completed or the courtship has resulted in marriage, for example. However, if you have chosen a story that is less narrative-driven, a story that focuses on the inner life and inner conflicts of a character, it is more likely that the story will end when the character reaches some insight that changes him or where equilibrium is regained.

In both cases, the external conflict focusing around the precipitating event, will lead to other external events which loosely will form a chronology for the story.

The dramatic strength of the story, however, will rest with how far, as writers, we are willing to explore the inner life of the characters.

In this sense the radio drama is far from the television drama, where the narrative chronology that follows the precipitating event is the heart of the story.

A radio drama may be intended for broadcast as a series or as a single event. Considerations of broadcast format as well as the nature of the audience will influence the structure of the drama.

If the play will be a series, you should develop discreet subthemes that will occupy each episode and give each episode its own integrity, dramatically.

Even if the drama will be broadcast whole, it is wise to break the play down into acts that reveal different aspects of the story, all the while moving the story along (more indirectly than television drama) towards its conclusion.

One of the strengths of radio drama is the imaginative possibilities to dramatize facets of the character's inner life—memory, desire, and fear. To do so, the writer can move back in time or forward. And in these flashbacks or flashforwards, the writer can set scenes that dramatize a feature of the character's inner life. This is the type of scenic opportunity where the writer can show us how a character would like to act rather than upon a reflection of how they did act. This freedom amplifies our sense of insight into the character and also shares a private moment with the character. In both cases, this type of scene makes the character fuller and more engaging for us.

CHARACTER

Strong characterizations are no less useful in radio drama than they are in television. But the writer has to characterize verbally rather than visually. The blind detective can be used on radio but the blindness and the manifestation has to be much more carefully articulated and that articulation requires verbalization and sound effects to allow the idea to resonate for the listener.

Consequently, it is easier in radio to rely on behavioral qualities that are more readily verbally articulated.

The use of dominant characteristics remains useful but they should rely more on verbal cues than on physical as in television.

And because we have only the audio avenue, you should try to simplify your characters as much as possible. Too much complexity can be confusing and you spend inordinate time characterizing rather than entering the inner life of the character.

What you want are strong, simplified characters.

Stereotypes serve you less well in radio drama than in television or film. Because the radio drama is less narrative-driven, the reliance upon our interest in the characters becomes more intense.

Beyond narrative concerns, the association of stereotypes with the absence of an inner life can lead to unexpected results, comedic, for example.

As a result what you want is strong, simplified, and fascinating characters.

In terms of the number of characters that is useful to your story, less is more. This would serve the principle of simplification in your story.

The most important, your main character, should be the focus of your efforts. Depending upon the story, you can have numerous manifestations of your main character—in the present, as a younger version, as an older version, as a manifestation of one aspect of his personality, the "wild side" of the 34-year-old retiring young adult earlier mentioned.

If you do present more than one version of the main character, try to avoid doing the same for the other characters. Clearly, the presentation of our character in scenes with his parents when all were younger contradicts this approach. In the main, this would be an exception. We want to avoid confusion; therefore presentations of the main character may vary, but the presentations of the other characters should remain constant.

LANGUAGE

What your characters say is almost everything in the radio drama. Consequently, the quality of that language has to be rich and leveled in its meaning.

You can choose a poetic or a naturalistic style but in both cases surprise, energy, and emotion have to pour from your words. These are high expectations indeed. But if you want to write radio drama this may be the single most challenging quality of the medium.

ECONOMY

Because a radio script is virtually 90% dialogue, writers can allow their language to run on. For the drama to work, this is not the right approach. In fact, like the short story, the form places particular expectations upon the language, the first being that the use of language be economic, compact, filled with meaning in few words.

For example, a character may speak about the passing of time. He is now 70 and not well. The character's goal is to make the point that time has flown by. He may speak about his youth, his marriage, his medical condition. He may refer to a sense of acceleration in time, as he became older. But when he talks about how he feels about time flying by, our character might say:

> "In my twenties, I felt I would live forever. In my thirties, I caught a flu that lasted six months. In my forties, I lost my wife to a richer man and my fifties, well, they just disappeared.."

In a very short paragraph the character tells us how he feels about time going by and he doesn't dwell upon numerous incidents, but rather in a compact way he tells us time has passed; indeed, recently it seems to have "disappeared".

Whatever you have your characters say, an economy of words is critical.

WIT

Besides economy, radio dialogue requires wit. Whether you define wit as cleverness, energy, or a form of verbal humor, you might consider wit, in part, to be all three.

At a deeper level, however, wit is an attempt by a character to cope with internal or external conflict. A character can use wit to keep his own equilibrium or to defuse conflict in a social setting.

The great playwrights of the century—Shaw, Beckett, Shepherd—understand the role of wit in the management of conflict.

Like humor in general, one dimension of wit is its relationship to aggression. But it is the other side of humor that is critical—the surprising or unexpected response to the aggression—a verbal response, a quick, short response, the verbal equivalent to the self-inflicted pratfall, the banana peel scene.

In order to animate language on radio, wit should be:

1. a surprise
2. aggressive
3. fast
4. short
5. clever

Going back to our example of a man feeling time has passed too quickly and now, at 70, he is reflective.

In this situation references to his last statement might be useful to coax out the potential for wit.

What he said was as follows:

"In my twenties, I felt I would live forever. In my thirties, I caught a flu that lasted six months. In my forties, I lost my wife to a richer man, and my fifties, well, they just disappeared."

The first pass at transposing this piece of dialogue into something more witty, suggests that the statement is too long. The dialogue needs to be broken down.

"At age 20, life was a curse. I was condemned.

At age 35, I became ill. But I lived. And I found the virtue of living.

At 45, my wife left me. I had lived too fully and she never forgave me. This time she would marry for money. She'd had enough of love.

When I was 55, I was condemned to die. A new curse. I experienced a
personal amnesia. I would block out the curse and carry on. And if I was quiet
about it, maybe no one would notice."

What to notice about the reworked piece of dialogue is that it is fragmented;
that it keeps twisting away from what you expect; that it has a dimension of aggression; and that it keeps energetic in spite of the nature of the struggle.

Clearly, the economic piece of dialogue in the first version has grown; it is
fuller in the second version.

Wit does not necessarily mean a loss of economy but to amplify the statement
with struggle or dramatic values and surprise, the statement is longer but presented in
a more fragmented form.

In presentation it would be important that it not be read as a full statement but
rather in clips. In this way the wit would not be lost in the larger statement. The
fragmentation helps keep the statement as a series of short bursts. This maintains the
energy within the statement.

IRONY

Wit is very much a present response; irony is more reflective, more comment
upon action than action itself.

Because the character's inner life is so important in the radio drama, so too is
the character's response to his inner life. I don't want to suggest that radio characters
are disembodied with souls wandering out there between the radio waves commenting upon their own behavior. But the character can ruminate upon himself, his situation, the character of others, or upon the situation.

This is where irony is so useful. Irony by its nature is conflictual and, consequently, it represents a mediating form of language between character and situation
or between inner life and outer action.

Irony can also be useful in presenting a transitional path out of a situation and
the opportunity to move along to the next point in the radio drama.

Going with our example of the 70-year-old commenting upon his life, a useful
ironic closing statement would be as follows:

"Just as I was beginning to get used to living, I have to begin to entertain the
idea of no longer living."

Think of irony as giving you the opportunity to comment on the state of the
character or situation.

OTHER SOUNDS

Sound effects and music are very important in creating context for the radio
drama. The main character may be a Russian soldier fighting at Borodino, but it is
the music and the effects that suggest the battle itself.

Whether the context be naturalistic or supernatural, sound and music will combine to create the critical ambiance for your story.

Consequently, the sound and music are tools that can be as important to you as heightened language.

All these factors have to come together to support the conflictual situation and to articulate the inner life and conflicts of your character.

FORMAT

The story is set in a mythical university. The main character is a young professor who is to be hired. The dean wants her to take initiative. Consequently, he doesn't assign her to specific teaching duties.

The scene that follows is the job offer.

1.	SOUND:	COFFEE BEING POURED.
2.	DEAN	Is your coffee all right?
3.	PROFESSOR	It's good.
4.	DEAN	Well, that's fine.
5.	PROFESSOR	The contract is acceptable.
6.	DEAN	I wish we could make you a better offer. I'm embarrassed but I have no choice.
7.	PROFESSOR	(inner monologue) He signs the checks and claims to have no choice. You probably have to memorize tripe like that to become Dean. As long as he doesn't pull the sexist, patronizing thing with me.
8.	PROFESSOR	You haven't told me the course I'll teach.
9.	DEAN	That's because I haven't assigned you teaching.
10.	PROFESSOR	But this contract hires me to teach.
11.	DEAN	Only if you sign it.
12.	PROFESSOR	I am planning to sign it.
13.	DEAN	What would you like to do?
14.	PROFESSOR	To teach.
15.	DEAN	I mean what would you really like to do?
16.	PROFESSOR	(inner monologue) Here it comes.
17.	PROFESSOR	What you're hiring me to do.
18.	DEAN	The modern university can't afford simply to teach. We have to be the temple of the technocracy.
19.	PROFESSOR	But I'm not a technocrat.
20.	DEAN	Then what are you?

The key dimension to the format is its simplicity. It highlights who is speaking and what they say. The dialogue is broken up here by inner monologue. Sound effects are mentioned briefly. In other scenes, effects might be more important. And certainly the addition of music will be important to create the background and emotional resonance for the story.

Writing radio drama is a challenge for the writer. Because of its concentration on language and on an inner life for its characters, the form is both imaginative and yet disciplined by the concentration on sound considerations to reach the audience. But it is also a very free form because it is not constrained by the naturalism inherent in visual media.

As a writer, this freedom poses a particular opportunity—to create a whole world for the ears and minds of your audience.

8

▼ Writing a Television
▼ Documentary

Television documentary embraces documentaries commissioned by specific television producers or stations, as well as documentaries produced independently and sold to television.

Generally television produces or buys documentaries that fall into very particular categories. The most common documentary falls into the general category of current affairs. In this sense the television documentary is very much related to journalism with relationships to newspapers and magazines.

Because of this relationship to journalism, the television documentary often has an investigative flavor to it. The story is ongoing. The documentary is a report on the story at this point.

It should come as no surprise then that the most important television documentary today is being produced by and for public television. Fred Wiseman's 6-hour documentary about an intensive care unit, entitled *Near Death* is a good example of this type of documentary.

The more popular manifestations of the documentary on commercial television is CBS's "60 Minutes." Other programs, "20/20" and "48 Hours" are offshoots of this popular program. In Canada, CBC's "The Journal" produces documentaries on this model.

That is not to say that all television documentaries are public affairs oriented. Not so many years ago, public television broadcast a long documentary called "The American Family" which chronicled the lives of members of the Loud family of California. Other documentaries have chronicled historical events: the Holocaust in *Shoah* and a personal search for history in *Sherman's March*.

The range of subject matter is broad but the majority of material broadcast on television relates to our lives in the same way that the daily issues in newspapers relate to our lives.

If you are commissioned to write a documentary for a particular show, the parameters will be fairly straightforward. But if you write an independent documentary the likelihood is that this chapter will have more relevance to you.

One more aspect about the role of the writer of documentaries is worth mentioning here. That is the role of the writer can differ considerably from project to project.

On many documentaries the challenging phase closest to writing is the research phase. Much of the interesting material, characters, and locations generate out of that research. Then the producer has a choice—to hire a writer or to write it himself.

Another way the documentary may evolve is from an idea rather than from a script. In this case the producer shoots a lot of footage and brings in a writer to help shape it at the editing stage. This approach, referred to as *cinema vérité,* obviously is far from perfect from the writer's perspective.

Consequently, the comments about documentary writing in this chapter are primarily relevant to writing prior to the production phase.

WHAT TYPE OF DOCUMENTARY

Are you writing a public affairs documentary or a personal documentary? If you are writing a public affairs documentary there are particular parameters you must meet.

1. Use only information that is verifiable.
2. Primary source material is more important than secondary source material.
3. Wherever possible, have participants speak for themselves (therefore use a narrator only when you have no other choice).
4. Acknowledge technical changes. For example, if you edit an interview and use only the first minute of a 30-minute interview, this should be acknowledged in some way. If it isn't, the documentary leaves itself open to the accusation of distorting the interview. Credibility is elusive but critical in the effectiveness of the public affairs documentary.

The Personal Documentary

The parameters for the personal documentary are not constrained in the same way.

As the writer, you can use the footage or other research material more freely. Indeed, interpretation is what makes the documentary personal. Credibility may be as much an issue in the personal documentary but not on the same factual basis as in public affairs.

In this type of documentary the role of the narrator as interpreter is central.

In between the public affairs documentary and the personal documentary, there is a range of documentary from social comment to biography. But in terms of features they fall into categories close to either the public affairs documentary or the personal documentary.

Point of View

As with the radio documentary the mode of interpretation is through a specific point of view.

Particular shows are known for their points of view. "60 Minutes" is investigative. Many shows on "20/20" are celebratory. Do you know the point of view used for your documentary?

If you don't know the point of view, you face a decision.

Having decided upon a point of view you face other practical decisions that relate to the visual dimension of the documentary.

The Interview

Head-on interviews can be a strong source of material in your documentary. We see the individuals you are interviewing and the visual relationship offers a chance to relate emotionally to them as well as to what they are saying.

This is so strong an option that there are documentaries that are primarily a series of "talking head" interviews.

Many writers and producers, however, opt for the other visual options to complement the interview material.

Location Shooting

Television provides you with the option of "being there." As a writer this has great potential. The sense of actuality, whether it be background material or central, is an exciting adjunct for the writer.

The basis for the location material is the research that you undertake. What you see can translate into an interpretive guide for the viewer. Don't be neutral. If you put what you see in the documentary our experience can only be richer for it.

Stock Footage

Whole companies exist on the proceeds of selling existing footage. Historical, geographical, people at carnivals, underwater footage, all this visual material is for sale and, from the writer's point of view, is a source of additional visual material.

This material becomes part of the documentary. To make it integrate, the narrator is the key.

As the writer, all sources, location, stock interviews as well as book sources are the raw material for your documentary. But because this is a visual medium, you, the writer, should keep an eye open to visual source material.

SHAPING THE MATERIAL

You are telling a story, albeit a story of actuality. In order to sort out the factual material, the presentation of your point of view is useful. As in radio, this should be done at the outset.

Having stated the subject and the point of view in the first sequence, you can begin shaping and organizing the sequences along the lines of making a case.

Each sequence should add to the case. If it does not, it simply repeats what another sequence has accomplished. Or worse, the sequence introduces a new idea too distant from the subject. The consequence is confusion and the creation of the idea that the viewer may be watching two distinct documentaries.

The sequences should be organized along a rising action. Attention should be given to making sure that the last sequence restates the case and makes the point conclusively, and with the greatest emotional impact of any of the sequences. In brief, the last sequence should be climactic.

In the television documentary, you have more opportunity to make sure the sequences in terms of features have commonalities with other sequences. Visual as well as aural connective elements include fragments from the same person being interviewed, similar locations, the presence of a narrator—all these give you options to refer to in the sequences when the viewer sees those people or places on a continuing basis across sequences.

Consideration should be given to including as much factual material as necessary to give the documentary credibility. But consideration should also be given to the emotional character of the documentary. An emotional connection to the people and ideas will strengthen the impact of your documentary.

Depending upon the type of documentary, the emotional component becomes more important relative to the degree of information. For example, in the documentary about a young girl who has a disabling condition, the National Film Board's *I'll Find a Way*, we need to know about the nature of the young girl's disability; but the strength of the documentary depends upon our emotional relationship with her and our admiration for her courage.

There are many ways to tell a factual story, but the impact is greatest when the emotional impact is strong.

IS YOUR MATERIAL STRONG ENOUGH

Television is a mass medium and its approach to material is not subtle. Consequently, the material best suited for television and the approach to that material is fairly extreme.

The material requires extreme credibility. But it also requires a treatment strong on dramatic values. The innocent man sitting in the death house; the bathing beauty, Miss America, who is a Ph.D. in physics; the world champion boxer who beats his wife; all of these stories are extreme. And consequently, they are factual stories that would be dramatically interesting to television audiences.

Television also naturally gravitates to crisis and disaster. Every day life per se is too quiet as material for television documentary. Few writers and producers have the courage to seek out real life drama and record it. Fred Wiseman in his work for PBS is one of the few. He makes films in high schools, hospitals, juvenile courts, basic training camps. But Wiseman is rare.

More often, television gravitates to those natural and unnatural disasters that propagate in our world. As a result there is no shortage of material for television documentaries.

THE IMPORTANCE OF THE CONTROVERSIAL

Because of our relationship with television, viewers are rapidly conditioned and numbed by documentaries recording disaster. Consequently, documentary producers more aggressively seek material that is increasingly controversial.

As a writer you will have to struggle with many ethical issues, but few will be as loaded as the issue of writing a documentary from the point of view of ferreting out the most controversial perspective upon the story.

As a writer you will have to decide. There is work one chooses to undertake and there is work one walks away from. This issue of conscience doesn't challenge your professionalism. Those of us who work in the media shouldn't forget that we are also citizens, husbands, fathers, lovers. All roles bring with them responsibility. No less for the writer, especially the writer of television documentary.

ALLOW THE RESEARCH TO LEAD YOU

What will save your work from drifting toward exploitation is the quality of your research. Not only is the research crucial to generate enough information to make the documentary credible, but research in its fullest sense will help you find incidents, characters, and facts that will surprise your audience and make the path of your documentary seem less linear.

For example, in the Maysles Brothers documentary on a Rolling Stones concert, *Gimme Shelter*, there is a long scene with the Stones' lawyer, famed Melvin Belli, who tries to negotiate a lease for Altamont, to hold the concert on that site. The business negotiations are far from the music of the Rolling Stones and yet the scene reminds us that rock concerts are big business with all sorts of beneficiaries beyond the musicians and the fans.

As a writer you should look for these surprising details that help flesh out your story, but that also surprise the audience.

There is a definite dramatic payoff in surprising details. These details can only be found in the research stage.

To go back for a moment to the relationship with journalism. The good journalist digs around for the story. So too the writer of the television documentary.

In many ways your script will only be as good as the quality of your research.

THE NARRATOR

The narrator on the television documentary can be anonymous as in the radio documentary, a person heard but not seen. Or the narrator can be an on-camera presence. On "60 Minutes" and "The Journal," the narrator is often an on-camera presence.

If this is the case, the narrator becomes, in effect, a character in the narrative. Indeed, the narrator becomes the central character, the person we identify with and through whom we interpret the story.

The on-camera narrator changes the nature of the narration from third person (potentially objective) to first person, subjective. The narrator becomes advocate, interpreter, explorer. He or she becomes our eyes as well as our ears.

Some documentaries such as the cinema vérité work by Fred Wiseman totally sidestep the narrator. What you see and hear is what you, the viewer, have to interpret. This cinema vérité approach is fairly rare. More often, since documentaries are shot quickly, the narrator is necessary whether on screen or off.

Narrators can be objective sounding or looking or they can be advocates, passionate in voice and presence. Each makes for a different type of documentary experience. But as long as you, the writer, know who you are writing for, the quality of the work needn't be less in one case over the other.

And because the visual dimension is present, the quality of the verbal narration can be less precise than is the case on the radio documentary.

In fact, in the case of the on screen narrator, the visual character is probably at least as important as what he or she says.

As with the radio documentary, what is said organizes the ideas that carry the documentary. Consequently, the primary considerations for the audio narrator is clarity of the ideas and continuity to the flow of those ideas.

Heightened language is less important when the body language of the narrator tells so much about how to interpret what is being seen.

In this area your main decisions are two:

1. Do you need a narrator?
2. If yes, should the narrator be on screen or off screen?

If the narrator is on screen be aware that the narrator becomes a principal character in the story.

FORMAT

Generally the format can present in one of two ways—two column or three column. Each is a variation on the other. The visual and audio components are separate.

OPTION I
VISUAL   AUDIO

OPTION II
VISUAL   AUDIO   NARRATION

Option II audio includes interview material, sound effects, and music; leaving narration, given its importance, to appear in its own column.

In both options, the visual and audio line up in coordinates that relate to one another.

A sample will illustrate the format. In this example, narration and audio are integrated in a single column. (Option I)

TEENAGER USA, 1990

A Television Documentary

by _____.

for _____. (program station)

contact: your name

address

phone

SEQUENCE 1

VISUAL	AUDIO
1. A classroom. Attentive students. Focus on a young man adjusting his glasses.	Voice-over Teacher lecturing.
	Music begins, carries over this sequence.
2. A street corner. A wealthy looking student is buying drugs from a dealer.	Popular song. Energetic, nervous.
3. A young female gets ready for her semi-formal.	Phone rings.
	She calls out "I'm busy. Franny, you get it will you please?"
4. Attentive student in the first shot. He is working in a supermarket.	Supermarket noise.
5. A poor teenager walking the street, nothing to do.	Music continues.
6. Young woman dancing at the semi-formal.	Narrator: These are today's teenagers—energetic, nervous, concerned about their future Wondering if they have a future. This report will look into what they think, what they think about us, about themselves, and how they feel about the future

END OF SEQUENCE.

Visually we have presented the idea that this will be a portrait, not of one, but of a cross section of teenagers.

And the narrator presents the point of view. It is investigative. In the course of this documentary we will find out what teenagers think about the future. Since they are the next generation that will come to power in the United States, what they think and how they feel about the future is very important.

The approach that I've just described is a straightforward one that would be suitable for an audience of parents.

How could I as a writer make this more appealing to the teenage audience itself? This means a more entertaining, provocative opening.

I would be tempted to open with a few excerpts from famous films about teenagers. For example, the rebellious Marlon Brando in *The Wild One* recording his rebelliousness when he says, in response to what he is rebelling against, "What have you got?" This excerpt would capture the teenage rebelliousness of the 1950's just as the famous sequence in the 60's film *The Graduate* where Benjamin, when asked what he wants to do now that he has graduated, responds that he doesn't know. The questioner suggests "plastics," there's a lot of money in plastics. This scene captures the naivety of the 60's teenager and his rejection of material values.

Appropriate sequences from the 70's and 80's films will trace the drift back to material goals and conformity.

Together these four excerpts suggest in a very entertaining way what teenagers were like in each era. Now the question is posed—what will they be like in this last decade of the twentieth century?

As the writer, you have numerous options. Knowing who your audience will be will help you choose the most appropriate options.

Now, onto the drama...

9

Writing a TV Drama

Television drama is a broad category that will concern us for the next four chapters. Each chapter will examine a popular dimension of television drama. In this chapter we will concern ourselves with the TV movie.

TV movies resulted from the success of Hollywood films broadcast on network television. As their popularity increased, and more films were shown, less films were being produced. The Hollywood library was being depleted. And so television turned to producing its own movies specifically for network broadcast. It is hard to believe that 25 years ago there was no such thing as a TV movie. Today there are categories of TV movies—star vehicles, women's films, teenage stories, issue oriented stories, docudramas, and miniseries.

Often miniseries (from 4 to 30 hours) are based on best-selling novels. TV movies more often are original screenplays based on headline events of issues, on the lives of celebrities, political and cultural, and as star vehicles that may become series if the TV movie is a success.

AUDIENCE

Few areas of television are as specifically targeted to audience as the TV movie. The reason is simple. The competition for the TV film are those feature films that appear first in theaters, then pay TV, and finally on network and local television.

Consequently, the TV movie has more competition than most areas of programming. The answer to the situation is to produce TV movies for target audiences.

Those target audiences are specific age and gender groups. Clearly, star vehicles should appeal across age and gender barriers, but even this consideration depends upon the star.

It is easier to look at the successful TV movies and identify films such as "The Burning Bed" and "Roe vs Wade" as women's films. A similar approach identifies a David Soul film or a Cheryl Ladd film as a star vehicle. Only the miniseries "Lonesome Dove," "War and Remembrance" or "Rich Man, Poor Man" develop out of best-selling novels. And here the assumption is that the scale of the story together with the success of the novel ("Lonesome Dove" was a Pulitzer Prize-winning novel) will assure a market for the miniseries.

Who the audience is may be the most important single criteria for the production of a television film.

LENGTH

In spite of the average miniseries length being 6 hours (lengths range from 4 to
30 hours), the more common length for a TV movie is 2 hours.

Two hours is the length that you, the writer of the TV drama, will have to work
with. In the balance of this chapter, the assumption is that you will be working with a
2-hour length.

The question that arises out of this length relates to the dramatic potential of
your story. Are the characters strong enough? Is there enough story to last 2 hours
(you need approximately 100 minutes of screen time for the 2-hour period). Is the
central conflict of your story meaningful to the target audience? Is your secondary
story line helping your major story? Is there enough action? We now turn to these
concerns.

THE IDEA

Your target audience is a teenage audience. The idea is based on a real life
event. Two boys at a private school go to visit the home of the richer of the two
boys. The other young man actually is a scholarship student from a middle class
family. The visit is a shock to the young middle-class boy. And during the visit the
boys get into trouble. There is a rape, a murder, and the accused is the middle-class
boy. The accuser is the other boy.

This story examines private school life but also the differences between middle-
class values and upper-class values. Is the middle-class boy victim or aspirant? Was
the murder his initiation into the fraternity of the rich? The story examines all of
these dimensions of the story.

Critical to the viability of the idea is that it presents in an unsubtle way a compelling story that carries us into a concern in our own lives.

In the idea proposed, the lives of privileged young men attract the young
middle-class boy. He wants to belong, but he doesn't know how. The implicit question is the ethical question. How much are you willing to give up to join the club of
privilege? And is it worth entering the club at any price?

The idea has lots of story—the private school, the middle-class boy's home life,
the rich boy's home life, the visitation; the rites of passage—the rape and murder,
capture, the accusation, and finally the trial and its outcome.

This is sufficient story for 2 hours. The question you should ask yourself continually is not only, Is there enough story? but also the question, Is my story compelling?

CHARACTER

The first question you should ask yourself is, Whose story is this?
In the idea put forward the person who is best positioned for the drama is the

middle-class boy. If the main character were a reporter digging around for the story, or the parent of either boy, we would be removed from the pain of the main story.

Even if the main character were the rich boy, we would be taking the "accuser" as the focus of the drama. The "victim" is a greater dramatic dilemma and has more potential for dramatic exploitation. The rich boy would probably make a better antagonist than protagonist in the story as put forward.

The second question you should ask yourself about character is whether there are possibilities to empathize with the main character.

Given that the character may be a killer, there could be difficulty empathizing with him. But given the polarities—differences in wealth, status, and possibly in the portrait of the two families, we might be able to, relatively speaking, empathize with the middle-class boy.

This will pose a particular challenge for you as the writer but the character is positioned in the story to garner some sympathy.

A third question you should consider is the relation of the main character to the secondary characters.

Important secondary characters include the rich boy, the two families, the victim of the crime, the middle-class boy's girlfriend. Of less importance but as characters with potential, siblings of both boys, the school master at the private school, the middle-class boy's former teacher, the investigators, lawyers, police.

All these characters have potential to help the story. But what is critical is that these characters line up along lines of two ethical choices for the boy—totally unethical or ethical. Clearly, the pivotal character is the rich young man. But other characters can and should be almost as significant.

Every effort should be made to differentiate the characters in terms of physical and behavioral characteristics.

THE GOAL

You have a situation and a group of characters. Now what is the goal of the story?

Do you want to emphasize the action of the story? Do you want to show the making of a murderer? Do you want to emphasize the link between money and immorality?

You have to be very precise about your goal because just as your point of view is the filter to help viewers interpret information in the documentary, your goal will help you organize the drama.

Without a goal you could easily drift and a lack of emphasis on one of the aforementioned goals will result in the watering down in impact of your drama.

Particularly with strong material (as with this story) the goal will help us enter the story and stay with your drama.

CONFLICT

As I've mentioned earlier, television is a medium which needs to hold your attention. If it doesn't you will leave, have a sandwich, go to a movie. If you stay, producers and station managers want you to stay with their show on their channel.

The level of conflict (which differs from the level of violence) will help maintain the viewer's interest in your story.

The story of these two boys has a lot of conflict. Their wealth, the differences in their backgrounds, their goals are the beginning of conflict.

The events of the story, the rape and murder, are another level of conflict.

Finally, the accusation of one boy by the other and the consequent prosecution of the case are another.

Conflict between characters, between characters and situations, as well as internal conflicts experienced by characters because of their past; or issues arising out of the conflict in their past clashing with present opportunities; all layer the story and keep us, the viewer, in a state of tension about how the conflict will be resolved.

It is critical that your story have enough conflict as a story but also a frequency of conflict to address the particular character of television.

THE MAJOR STORY LINE

The major story line in television is frequently the action line, that series of events that carry the main characters toward a climax.

In our story, the events of the major story line include: the main character arrives at private school; he has no friends; he is befriended by the rich boy; their friendship develops; the rich boy invites the main character to his home for a weekend; they travel to the rich boy's home; they go out for an evening; they pick up a girl in the local town; they drive her to a secluded place; the evening ends for the middle-class boy when he passes out from too much drink; they travel back to school; school life; the middle class boy is arrested; he is interrogated; he finds out his accuser is the rich boy; he is to be tried; the trial; the outcome.

The major story line concerns itself with the major plot developments, but not necessarily story aspects that characterize the main characters.

THE MINOR STORY

The minor story concerns itself entirely with character.

In this story, we gain insight into the main character's other life—his original life.

In this story he has a family, a decent family, and a girlfriend. It is the girlfriend who is afraid of losing him, now that he is going to a private school and getting a chance to meet lots of rich girls. The story of their relationship throughout his troubles forms the basis for the minor story line.

She represents his past and maybe his future. Certainly his present circumstances, a young man accused of rape and murder, suggest not only challenges to their relationship but also raise the question whether he will have any future.

The role of the minor story is to give some dimension to the main story. Usually the minor story line adds a human or more emotional dimension to the story.

It is critical that the minor story line not repeat the dramatic intentions of the main story. It should be different but related to the main story through the common denominator, the main character.

There will come a point towards the end when the two stories merge, but for your purposes it is best to consider them separate and to think of them as complementary to one another.

Both are necessary to the success of your TV drama.

ARE YOUR SECONDARY CHARACTERS APPROPRIATE

Your secondary characters should be placed to advance the story or highlight some aspect of the main character's personality. This can be a contrast or a similarity.

And you should have an antagonist who deepens the plight or heroic opportunity for the main character. In both cases, the role of the antagonist can help the dramatic quality of your story.

In our story, the best protagonist–antagonist combination is the two classmates. The rich boy, because he becomes the accuser and witness of his former friend and classmate, is an excellent antagonist. Because we don't see the murder on screen, he may even be the real killer or an accomplice. Consequently, he remains appropriately mysterious and aggressive.

Among the other secondary characters, the girlfriend and the victim are both very important. They represent the opportunities for behavior we would deem "good" and "evil" with regards to the actions of the main character.

The two young women, members of each boy's family, the mothers and fathers, are important. They provide the context to consider the moral–immoral dimension of the behavior of the two boys. Where did the capacity to kill come from?

Beyond these key secondary characters numerous people fulfill plot functions —lawyers, police, classmates, the school master.

The question you should ask yourself about the secondary characters is whether they are helping you tell your story. The secondary characters I've described here all fulfill that criteria.

DO YOU HAVE ENOUGH VISUAL ACTION

The medium is first visual, and as the writer, you have to recognize the visual possibilities when you tell your story. What you are trying to avoid is the opposite; a story mired in dialogue.

In order to take advantage of visual opportunity (budgetary tolerated opportunity), you should first attempt to develop a sense of the visual opportunity in key locations—the private school, the rich boy's home, the rich boy's town (relative to the middle-class boy's home and town), the location where the killing takes place, the jail, the courtroom.

Where possible, you should set action or reveal character in situations of action. For example, the first time the middle-class boy attends class at the private school, where he sits, how the teacher interacts with him, and how the other students react to him is one thing. But how he reacts could be quite another.

Milieu, behavior, reaction all offer the writer an opportunity to rely less on dialogue and to take advantage of visual opportunity.

THE DANGER OF TOO MUCH DIALOGUE

Even if your dialogue is wonderful, you are always in danger of relying on dialogue too much.

It is always easier to say what a character is like than to show what he is like.

Similarly, with advancing the plot, it is always easier to say what should happen next rather than to show it. Particularly when they don't have enough time for the job, writers fall back on dialogue.

The danger of using too much dialogue is also audience-related. Television is a medium that relies on maintaining the viewer's interest. That means his visual and aural involvement.

The consequences of this claim manifests itself in more ways than visual action and quick dialogue. It also means that scenes are shorter and that writer's tend to get to the point more quickly than they would otherwise.

In general terms, using too much dialogue is symptomatic of the full range of problems suggesting the writer is not playing to the medium. Television and pace, fast pace, are almost synonyms. The message then, is don't use too much dialogue in your story.

STRUCTURAL OPTIONS

When telling your story you should try to find the structure that is most useful, given your goal.

If your goal is the crime and the merit of punishment to suit the crime, then you should begin the story during the trial. The middle-class boy is on trial for his life.

By beginning the story in this fashion and telling the rest of the story through the perspective of witness (and then, in effect, flashbacks) the frame of the story and, implicitly, the goal is crime and punishment.

If, on the other hand, you want to emphasize the clash of values and the idea that things go wrong when you go against your values and try to adopt another's values, the structure should be framed closer to the family lives of the two boys. In relative terms these sequences would be more important relative to those sequences revolving around the crime and subsequent trial.

Besides the straightforward structure of telling the story chronologically, which would not give as much weight to either of the two goals mentioned earlier, there is yet another option. We could structure this story as a Romeo and Juliet story with the class issue separating the two families. In this version, the girlfriend becomes more important and may be the subject of some rivalry between the two boys. In this scenario the rape and murder are tests of the degree to which one of the boys will go to destroy the rival.

Here we move far from the original parameters of the story. It could be a viable structure to explain the tragedy. In this version the murder, and particularly the subsequent trial, is less important than building up the triangle between the two boys and the girlfriend.

The important point here is that you, as the writer, have numerous paths or structural options available. Each option results in a somewhat different story. The basic story elements however remain the same.

THE COMPELLING APPROACH TO THE COMPELLING STORY

In writing a TV movie, your job as writer is to find a compelling approach to what you have decided is a compelling idea.

Such is the power of the medium that you are enlisted as writer to match it with your power as storyteller.

Everything has to proceed quickly in the most effective manner, all the while knowing that the viewer can change that channel on you.

If a writer ever needs a burst of energy for his work, that channel fickleness will do it every time.

You must write in the most compelling manner if you are to go on writing for television.

Format

```
                          TITLE


              by  _____.


             for  _____.
           (TV program or Production Company)
```

1. It is raining, a thunderstorm. A young man, BRAD, walks to his mailbox. He opens the box with much anticipation. He removes one letter. What he's been waiting for. He opens it. The rain is falling like a sheet. He can barely read but he notices the words "pleased to offer you..."

He stuffs the letter into his pocket and begins to run.

                    BRAD
    Mom! Dad! I'm in! I'm in!
    He runs and is lost in the hail that begins. But we can hear
    his voice. Brad is a happy man.

CUT TO:
2. INT. KITCHEN – DAY
Brad's MOTHER is stirring the soup. He is soaked to the skin.

                    MOTHER
    You'd better get out of those clothes or you won't live to go
    to that fancy school.

                    BRAD
    It's not fancy. It's just good.

                    MOTHER
    Good and fancy.

                    BRAD
    Good.

                    MOTHER
    They won't make you soup like this.

                    BRAD
    You can mail me some every week.

                    MOTHER
    Now you're making fun of me. Wait till you're up there.
    You'll probably think of me and your dad as sources for your
    humor. I hope you won't forget us, Brad.

                    BRAD
    I haven't left yet, Mom.

                    MOTHER
    And don't forget where you came from, son, don't forget.
                    END OF SCENE.

    Now we're going to leave the TV movie and move on to comedy writing, an-
other form of important storytelling on television.

10

Writing a Situation Comedy

Writing a situation comedy is not quite as easy as it might appear. In fact writing comedy is the most difficult form of writing for television.

The reason is straightforward. You have to tell a credible, involving story with all the attendant dramatic values. And the story has to be funny.

Funny for most television situation comedies means verbal humor rather than visual (although there is a role for visual humor). But verbal humor isn't simply someone telling a joke; it means a remark or reaction arising out of a dramatic situation. The writer has to make sure to set up the dramatic situation. If this doesn't happen, the viewer is faced with the situation where the characters are telling jokes to one another and implicitly to us. This is not what you want to happen to your story.

In this chapter we will take up the issue of humor and drama and detail the ingredients you need to write a successful half hour situation comedy (actually 23 minutes of script).

WHAT IS FUNNY?

In Chapter 7 in a discussion of wit, I suggested that wit requires a surprise and the presence of aggression. It is the response of a character that is surprising and witty.

Humor comes from a parallel but broader situation.

A dramatic situation is filled with conflict. One response to that conflict is intense emotion. A more surprising response can be humor. Humor has conflict, aggression, and surprise. The upshot of the surprise is that we laugh. The laughter is a release of tension (the character's and our own). The key terms are conflict and surprise.

Humor can be verbal, it can be visual, it can take a higher form (wit), or a lower form (farce); it can be outer-directed (satire) or it can be self-directed.

When it doesn't work, humor can easily be viewed as bullying or embarrassing.

If it is on target, we laugh; if is isn't we cringe!

If you make sure to set the situation in dramatic terms, and make the character's response a surprise rather than premeditated, the likelihood is that the response will be funny.

One other element. There are characters who use humor as a shield and an avenue to interact with others (and the world at large). They are the clowns, the fools that know their place and role in the world. And they are funny.

They are useful characters in your stories because we more naturally accept and understand why and when they use humor.

These characters often will populate situation comedies (not entirely but to an unusual degree). Get comfortable with this type of character, especially if you are going to write situation comedy. And realize that these characters are a part of all of us; more so in good comedy writers.

REAL SITUATIONS

It is important in developing your story that you use a realistic approach. Fantasy is a special form; so too is satire; both are exaggerations beyond realism. Situation comedy develops out of real life situations with recognizable characters. The dramatic values have to be strong and believable. It is the point of view that creates the comedy.

As a result, you will have to attend to the dramatic values of your situation comedy as much as you would to other forms of dramatic writing. In fact, the success of the comedy will depend upon how believable you have made your story.

Real situations are the starting point for situation comedies.

POINT OF VIEW

What distinguishes the situation comedy from a drama is the point of view.

In the drama the build up of tension in a scene is intended to increase our empathy with the main character and his or her situation. In a comedy the intention is not empathy. The buildup of tension in a scene is diverted visually or by language to a target, the characters themselves, or the opposition.

For example, the scene is as follows:

A blind man, cane in hand, is walking down a street. It is a one-way street and he is walking the wrong way. Cars are driving right by him. In a dramatic scene a driver stops, puts him in the car and drives off. Empathy is present and the tension is over.

The same scene. Different point of view. The blind man is walking down the street. The first car comes at him and swerves to avoid him. He walks on. The second car has witnessed what has happened. He will not be humiliated by a pedestrian. He drives as if he were playing chicken. He is driving right at the blind man. The blind man doesn't veer from his course. The second driver finally veers off.

A third driver now comes at the blind man. And he is even more annoyed. He will not be deterred. At the last instant before impact, the blind man trips over a stone and falls out of the way. He is saved by his blindness. And again he has avoided disaster. The third driver rushes from his car and grabs the blind man. He shakes him and says, "Just because you're blind doesn't mean you should take over the road!" The blind man just stands before him. He shakes his head and tugs at his ear. It is apparent he can't hear either!

This brings us to the last component of humor. It has to be a surprise, a twist of our expectations. A blind man who is deaf is a surprise. Just as a blind man not being victimized by sighted men in cars is a surprise.

Point of view is critical together with aggression in the development of humor in a scene.

OPPOSITES

Just as the blind man and the car driver are opposites to one another, you should use opposites to create characters who have comic potential.

Think of "The Odd Couple," "Golden Girls," the father and son in "Family Ties": all are extreme opposites. The use of characters who are at either end of an extreme spectrum gives you the gap between them as areas of comic potential. And their expected extreme response to a given situation will be the exact opposite of the other character. This differential provides the aggression for the scene. [Whenever individual goals differ, one person will will win and the other will lose in a scene. What is important to the writer is not who wins or loses but rather, the conflict generated, assuring the presence of aggression in a scene.]

You might ask the question if the characters are known to be opposite to one another, we know their responses in a given situation. So where is the surprise?

The surprise has to be in the development of the story. On a recent show one of the characters in "Golden Girls" thinks she may have contracted AIDS from a blood transfusion. Not a very funny subject. And the character is the most religious morally unambiguous of the three. Even less funny. But in the response of this character to her situation, she is uncharacteristic. She is afraid but she is manic, more active than ever. She is not restrained as she usually is. And how this quality affects her housemates is the source of the humor in the episode.

Opposites in characters as well as situations is a critical basis for the development of humor.

THE ROLE OF EXAGGERATION

Another source of humor beyond opposites is exaggeration.

In a realistic situation, our anticipation is that a character's response will be predictable. As in life, this isn't always the case.

One option for the character is an exaggerated response. One example of an exaggerated response is the drivers' response to the blind man walking towards them as they drive. This is an exaggerated behavioral response.

An example of a verbal exaggeration is the traditional "If you were on a desert island. . . " When asked what food the character would take along, the character says a freezer full of frozen french fries. Asked why, he responds that there are no fast food outlets on the island. There is more than one exaggeration here.

An exaggeration in a more recognizable circumstance is as follows. Two teen-agers are speaking around the issue of going out together. The following exchange takes place.

>   FRANK
>   I'd like to go to a baseball game. It's been awhile...
>
>   ANNETTE
>   I hate baseball.
>
>   FRANK
>   Do you like basketball?
>
>   ANNETTE
>   No.
>
>   FRANK
>   Is there any sport you think I could take you to?
>
>   ANNETTE
>   Pie eating.
>
>   FRANK
>   I understand you like to be a participant, not an observer.
>
>   ANNETTE
>   No, I just don't like uniforms.

The reference to pie eating is an exaggeration used to make a point. It is a sur-prise and it helps develop verbal humor.

Exaggeration can be an important source of humor in your teleplay.

THE HALF HOUR

The usual length for the sitcom, as it is more often referred to, is 23 minutes (at a page per minute, the expectation is that you turn in a 23-page script).

That may not seem like much but remember that you have to tell a story, in fact two stories. And you have to produce a script that will generate much laughter. Twenty-three minutes is a lot of laughs.

STRUCTURE

Your script should consider the following structure:

1. Tease
2. Act I
3. Midpoint
4. Act II
5. Climax
6. Epilogue

In the course of this structure you should use four elements to fashion the script.

1. The established characters for the show
2. A problem
3. A major story
4. A secondary or minor story

In order to consider structure first in a general sense, let's turn to the characters and the story.

THE CHARACTERS

As mentioned earlier, the characters should have been originally developed with much consideration to opposites. The "capitalist" son and the "hippy" father in "Family Ties," the fastidious Felix and the messy Oscar in "The Odd Couple" are two examples.

But there are many other variations of the use of opposites—the grandfather/ grandchild, the butler/father, the black/white, the divorced/married, and so on.

You develop characters that will serve the idea, and often the characters and ideas, if the show is successful, become inseparable.

Consequently, when you write you should know those characters very well and use their qualities in their stories. How often was Mary's character in "The Mary Tyler Moore Show" challenged by a situation that used her conservatism and personality as a foil to the situation? Perhaps no show better illustrated this tension than the death and funeral of Chuckles the Clown. This is the show where Mary can't stop laughing during the funeral oration (hardly a conservative response). The moment is painful and funny and it implies the next important point about character.

Good comic writing allows the main character to make a fool of herself. Mary does it during the funeral.

Remember that the fool, just as the clown, is an honored comic persona. And very often characters, main and secondary, slip into a situation for which they are not prepared. The outcome is very often comic. But it is you, the writer, who has to be willing to let your characters on occasion play the fool.

THE PROBLEM

Situation comedies are stories about real people in real life situations. Since the show is weekly, we can't just visit a wonderful group of people every week. We need a shaping device for each show. The shaping device is the problem.

The problem usually presents itself as an issue—in the teenage show, getting a date for the semi-formal, or more seriously, a teenage pregnancy in the class. In the more adult shows, like "The Mary Tyler Moore Show," it is dealing with death or a promotion or a new relationship. The problem presents itself as a challenge for the main character and the show ends in the resolution of how the main character deals with the issue.

This is somewhat different from the TV movie where the main character actually grows through a change substantial enough to suggest resolution.

Because the half hour sitcom has set characters it is more appropriate to think of the main character accepting or becoming accustomed to a new situation rather than going through the type of change one sees in longer TV dramas.

THE MAJOR STORY

There are two story lines in every half-hour sitcom. Each story is associated with a different character. And each story presents a particular dilemma for that character.

The major story is related directly to the problem. A character thinks he may have AIDS. Another character has to face up to the fact he can't read. And yet another character has decided that after 6 years at one job, she is going to try for a promotion.

The major story line is defined by the problem. And the story is over when the problem is resolved; the character doesn't have AIDS or faces up to his reading problem and begins to learn, and so on.

THE MINOR STORY

Another character has a particular goal that seems a challenge (and happens to have some relationship to the major story).

For example, the major story line relates to teenage pregnancy. A minor story line would relate to an important date for another character. In both stories dating was a phase of the relationship. In the major story line we are at a late stage of the relationship. In the minor story line we are at the beginning of a relationship (which may or may not survive its beginning).

Late in the script the two stories can come together. They don't have to wrap up at the same point. In fact, the minor story doesn't have to resolve itself as definitively as the major story.

The point of using a major and a minor story line is to give two perspectives; a layering that will make the major story seem less linear and create a situation where two characters are conflicted rather than one. It also avoids a situation where all but one character react only to the way the main character is dealing with the problem.

By using a major and minor story line, the dramatic opportunities are greater and when conflict is greater, so too the possibilities for humor.

THE TEASE

At the beginning of the show there is a brief scene which is the equivalent to the warm-up to the show.

It is quick and must be funny. Generally it involves the interaction of at least two characters.

Some shows, which are moving to a more realistic format and approach, have done away with the tease, which is certainly a holdover from variety television and, before television, from vaudeville.

In a sense it is like a small routine. Because of its brevity, the emphasis is on the laughs.

Act I

In Act I, the problem is set and both the major and minor story lines begin.

To the extent that it is possible, all the important secondary continuing characters are used in this act, as they are throughout.

The story has to progress with plot complications and we have to move the action to the midpoint, which for the main characters means a confrontation with the party who is perceived to be the main barrier.

In the story when Mary Tyler Moore wants a promotion, this means progressing toward a meeting with her boss, Lou Grant.

In Act I she will deal with her colleagues, all of whom have different views about promotion and who should be their boss. Should they be promoted? They too could use the money (Murray). And what of those who already make more than she does, i.e., Ted. How does he feel if Mary were to make as much as he does?

Their ambivalence adds tension to her decision to see her boss.

THE MIDPOINT

Halfway through (just before the commercial) Mary faces a crisis—she sees Lou and asks him for the promotion. He laughs. He never could see her in any other way but as Mary, doing what she has been doing.

This confrontation which makes the character, Mary, feel like a fool, is a setback, a crisis.

The midpoint provides us a high intense note to end Act I; it points the direction for Act II. How will she deal with the rejection? Will she insist on being taken seriously or will she accept her situation?

The function of the midpoint is to bring the story to its first crisis. The high point helps shape the entire script in that it shapes Act I (the climax) and it points the direction for Act II. In this sense it sets up the approach to the climax at the end of Act II.

Act II

Act II is not only the response of the character to the crisis generated in the midpoint scene, it also provides a resolution to the problem (the climax).

Since the secondary characters are already introduced in Act I, their presence isn't new and invigorating.

But it is the minor story which was introduced in Act I that can swing into more important dimensions in Act II, and help move the major story toward the climax.

Generally it is the interaction of the character of the minor story line who interacts with the major story line and that interaction turns the main character around—to accept her plight or to insist on a change.

THE CLIMAX

The climax consists of the same characters who were present in the midpoint—think of them as protagonist and antagonist. But this time the main character is better equipped to deal with the situation. Some success—temporarily promoted—could provide a resolution and a successful climax.

The key dimensions of the climax is that it resolves the problem posed in Act I.

EPILOGUE

There is usually a brief funny epilogue after the climax.

The point of this is that even if its funny, the climax is loaded dramatically and it's too intense to leave the story on.

Consequently, a brief visually funny epilogue involving one of the two characters who have been central in the major and minor story lines, is what is used.

The epilogue is the visual equivalent of a punch line. It is light and it is funny and it leaves the audience with a laugh, the last note appropriate in a situation comedy.

FORMAT

One potential format you can use for the situation comedy is the same format as the one used for the TV movie.

There is, however, another format which I will use here.

The TV movie format is appropriate for a filmed sitcom. More often a sitcom is filmed or videotaped on a studio set. To make the taping economical, videotaping proceeds with three cameras recording the scene from a different angle. The final show is edited using the material from these three different cameras (long, medium, close). Pick-ups or close-ups are often picked up in the repeat of a particular scene.

This a roundabout way of saying that the script format for three cameras is a different format. And it is the format included here.

This type of format results in a script–time relationship of 2 pages per minute. The result is that a 23-minute script would be approximately 45 pages or more.

```
                         SCRIPT TITLE
              by  _____.
              for three camera videotaping.


First Draft.
```

```
                    for TITLE OF SHOW
                contact:   name.
                           address.
                           phone.
```

Act I

```
Fade in: Int. Living Room—Night
```

Jack is fixing himself a drink. He sits down in front of the television. His wife, Janis, walks in.

>   JANIS
>   The kids are asleep. We're alone at last.

HE CLICKS ON THE TELEVISION.

>   JACK
>   You, me, and the San Francisco 49'ers.

>   JANIS
>   I've waited for this since the Super Bowl.

THE TELEPHONE RINGS.

>   JACK
>   It couldn't be my bookie. The game's not over yet.

>   JANIS
>   I'll get it.

SHE ANSWERS THE PHONE. JACK IS EXCITED BY THE PREGAME WARMUP.

>   JANIS
>   Jack, forget the game. We've got to go.

>   JACK
>   Not unless there's a fire.

>   JANIS
>   It's your father, Jack. He's had a heart attack.

END OF SCENE.

In the last line, the problem is set up. In the balance of the show the major story line will be how Jack deals with his father's heart attack.

The situation comedy is one of the staples of commercial television. It has been important since the days of "I Love Lucy" and it is just as important now, in the era of Bill Cosby.

If you have an affinity for humor, situation comedy writing will appeal to you. It is great fun. Enjoy it.

11

▼ Writing a Soap Opera
▼
▼
▼
▼

The soap opera, a popular form of television drama, has in the past 15 years broadened from a phenomenon of interest to an audience primarily of women, to a broad based popular form.

The soap opera has been so popular in fact that it has jumped from afternoon programming to prime time evening. "Dallas" and "Dynasty" are based in content and style on the afternoon soap opera. And "Hill Street Blues," in terms of form, follows the soap opera model. More recent shows, "L.A. Law" and "thirtysomething," have also been influenced by the soap opera.

Our concern in this chapter will be the afternoon soap opera—"The Young and the Restless," "Santa Barbara," and their predecessors, which generally are seen in 1-hour segments.

As with every situation comedy or any other continuing series, each series will have a "bible" which details the concept for the series, the continuing characters, the type of stories that would be suitable, and the dos and don'ts for the series. This is important for writing a soap opera because each soap opera has particular direction. Without a knowledge of that direction, or where your episode comes into the story, you, the writer, would be lost.

What follows presumes your knowledge of the show bible and where your show fits into the series.

To prepare for writing for the soap opera there are a number of general considerations I would like you to consider.

FOILS AND FOOLS

The soap opera is populated by a cast of characters who are not only extreme opposites, they are positioned in such a way that the characters are foils for one another.

This operating principle is applicable even within families. There is the good son and the evil son, the faithful mother, the unfaithful father, the rich cousin, the poor cousin, the religious aunt, and the immoral uncle.

Polarities do abound in the soap opera. But foils relate characters more directly to one another. The webbing between characters is as strong as is the fact that they are opposites.

Foils as characters allows for much in the way of plot possibilities. But where emotional connection with the characters occurs is when the writer allows the character to be a fool.

We can hate a fool and we can feel sorry for a fool. Both emotional responses are vital for a rapid emotional involvement with the plight of the characters.

Consequently, a willingness to allow a character to become pregnant, or lose all his money, or steal all of someone else's money, is important in the soap opera.

Seeing the characters in terms of foils or fools will help you write a soap opera.

A WORLD OF FEELING AND ACTION

In the soap opera people act and react. And they talk about how they feel in both situations.

The soap opera is a medium for the exploration of relationships, for trying to define one's place in the world, and for trying to understand the strains of having relationships, and making progress. Life is no linear experience! Indeed, it is filled with surprise, not always of a pleasing sort.

Consequently, feeling, and the articulation of feeling, is important. It is the way characters define their progress as well as the response to resistance to progress.

The characters in soap operas have an obsession for speech and contact. And they are always checking how other characters are feeling.

This is quite different than the TV movie or the sitcom or police story where characters have a problem that they resolve in the course of the drama. They act in order to resolve the problem.

Action is not as frequent in the soap opera; just as ventilating feeling is not as frequent on the other forms of teleplay.

Intense response and reportage of that response is an important quality unique to the soap opera.

LIFE'S MAJOR DILEMMAS

The raw materials of the soap opera are all the personal crises that we face in a lifetime—illness, loss, relationships, material well-being and its loss.

And where there are ambitious, attractive people whose goals conflict with one another, we also have avarice, jealousy, rage, even murder.

It is true that every once in a while there is a happy event—the birth of a baby for example. But as to not lull us into acquiescence and tranquility, the very next scene will pose the revelation the father isn't who you think it is. Who is the father? And how does the mother prevent the presumed father and the real father from meeting and facing off against one another?

The soap opera is filled with life crises. It is certainly an accelerated form of dramatic realism.

THE BEST AND THE WORST

And into this television world of life crises waltzes a cast of characters who are not only foils and fools, they are also the very best and the very worst of the players in the human drama.

The characters, when they are attractive, are the most attractive; and when they are repellent, they are the most repellent.

There is very little room for middle ground people. If one character is a wealthy businessman who is avaricious, there is nothing the man won't do to make more money. The best and the worst principle includes his behavior with his family as well as his business associates. He may be as greedy about love, and giving and receiving, as he is about his balance sheet.

In a way the characters in the soap opera are stereotypes set in more extreme form.

As a result, the antagonists in soap operas are genuinely evil. The result is that the protagonists in their efforts are more heroic for their capacity to overcome the antagonist.

The heroes are the best and the villains are the worst. This is part of the intensity of the soap opera.

WHAT'S THE PROBLEM?

In the world of soap operas, everyone has a problem. And if they don't have one today, they'll have one tomorrow.

There is an effort on soap operas to integrate issues of the day. Consequently, the problem for a day, a week, or longer, might be an environmental disaster or the arrival of a long lost cousin from Eastern Europe.

Or the problem may be less news-oriented. It may involve a new relationship or a new business deal.

There is another dimension to the problem. It doesn't resolve itself at the end of the episode. Indeed it should carry on for some time as an issue in the show.

What distinguishes the soap opera from other forms of teleplay is that there is more than one problem in any particular show.

It is best to think of the soap opera as four distinct stories, with four characters who face their own problems. The problems range from personal to practical. This provides many opportunities for intense conflict. But is also provides intersection points of different characters and their varying problems.

When two characters, given their agendas and the barriers to them (the problems), meet or coincide, the dramatic moment becomes more complex. These crossover points can provide act ends or midpoints or possibly a climax. But most important, these crossover points, as they occur, demarcate the rising action of the dramas throughout the course of the episode.

They also keep the rising action moving from show to show, since problems do not necessarily get resolved at the end of an episode.

The gain to working through four stories in one episode is that resolution is not possible or necessary by the end of the episode. The critical dimension, for the viewer, is the opposite. Like real life, the soap opera keeps on going, day after day. Resolution would contradict the raison d'être of the soap opera.

CHARACTER

To develop a cast of characters who have maximum flexibility for the soap opera, the following list will be helpful.

1. Use foils or opposites.

   Is your character honest or dishonest?

   Is your character expressive or evasive?

   Is your character a victim or a perpetrator?

2. Use stereotypes for quick recognizability. The audience wants to recognize your characters and link them with types in their own lives. Tags, verbal and visual, are helpful here.

3. Are you allowing for heroic action by a character? An extreme antagonist is useful here.

4. In order to allow for strong reaction to your characters, you should allow characters to make fools of themselves, and to allow them to indulge in their weaknesses.

5. The problem should have a suitable relatedness to the character. The prob lem is either a goal or a barrier to the character. The wider the gap between character and problem, the more suitable the problem.

The nature of your character may be the single most important quality of your teleplay.

STRUCTURE

The structure of the soap opera is a four act structure as follows:

1. Opening
2. Act I
3. Act II
4. Act III
5. Act IV
6. Climax

General comments about the structure are necessary.

In terms of the narrative, there are four stories each revolving around a character and his problem or goal. Each story has a rising action. What marks the soap opera and differentiates the form from other television dramas is that the principle of rising action has to carry on into the next episode. As mentioned earlier, this is one of the benefits of using four stories. If one resolves during the episode, you have three others continuing. And in the next episode you can introduce a fourth. The cycle keeps going on in episode after episode.

OPENING

The opening refers back to the climax at the end of the last episode. Often the last scene is reiterated with the introduction of a new perspective.

Just as often, the more recent soaps will use the opening to reiterate briefly a sense of where each story was left the previous day. In a sense, this means four openings of critical importance to the writer; the opening provides the connection between the last episode and the present episode. They also set up a preview of the direction for the present episode.

What the viewer should not know from the opening is which story will resolve today, if a story will resolve. One strategy that is helpful in developing the episode is as follows:

Act I

Act I sets up the major problem or the most emphasized problem and character for this episode. You can think of it as the dominant problem and character.

It is important in this act to sense the challenges of this problem for the character. In essence we need to see that the problem is more complicated than first anticipated by the character.

This affords the opportunity to entwine other characters and to move towards the introduction of two other characters and their problems. Both of these stories are just introduced in this act. Neither story is as serious or challenging as the dominant problem. They offer a contrast as well as the opportunity for the writer to use these other problems-characters as complications to the dominant problem.

So often the soap opera, from the writer's point of view, is the opportunity to introduce as many twists and turns as possible.

Although it may seem overly complex, it, in fact, isn't. Primarily because the emotional survival of the character is the goal and challenge (even when the problem is more pragmatic), writing a soap opera means staying close to character. Plotting per se is less critical than placing characters in stressful or compromised positions. The viewer is more interested in seeing how your characters will react than the achievement of their goals. As a result you don't have to hurry to that goal. You just have to make the trip as complicated, emotionally, as possible.

Act I should end with a crisis, usually arising out of the clash between a secondary character and his or her problem with the dominant problem and character.

Act II

In Act II, the issue of dealing with the crisis of Act I is played out.
There is conflict but also a compliance on the part of some characters which

gives the illusion of a fall off in the conflict. Indeed it may be that resolution of one problem seems possible. At least until the end of this act.

At the end of Act II another crisis develops suddenly and we are again enveloped in concern for the fate of the character at risk. This usually is not the dominant character problem, but rather one of the secondary characters.

It is important that the crisis be different from the crisis at the end of Act I. If the first crisis is based on a pragmatic issue or basis, then the crisis at the end of Act II should be personal. Because it is personal, it will give the illusion that more is at stake than was the case at the end of Act I. This is important because throughout the episode, there should be a growing sense of greater crisis and an impending sense of loss, even doom. Again the principle of rising action is at play.

Act III

The fourth story, problem and character, can be introduced in Act III. The introduction keeps us from emotional exhaustion—something new generates a sense of relief and curiosity.

In this act there is progress in at least two of the other stories. And the act ends with the cross section of the new story with the dominant problem-character. This could give some direction to Act IV. But it also should complicate the story even more. Instead of three people attempting to achieve oppositional goals, now we have four. And this particular world should never have felt so complicated.

Act IV

Act IV has to move us to that point, the climax, when the world really feels like its coming to an end.

Act IV should generate as much emotional overload as possible among the characters. And at least one should be at that point where they are either undone or swamped by the situation.

For the climax, you want the sense that someone has been washed overboard and tomorrow you, the viewer, will find out if he will live or be dead.

Heightened feeling and movement toward a climax is the agenda of Act IV.

CLIMAX

The climax, the end of the episode, should trap one character who is close to resolution vis-à-vis the problem. But suddenly they have never seemed farther from resolution.

Whether this is the dominant problem-character will depend upon the day of the week. Certainly on Fridays it should be the dominant character-problem (to help carry interest over the weekend). It is also typical of the last show of the season.

Uppermost in the choice is the degree of involvement between audience and show. Producers will usually have specific instructions for most shows but more for Friday shows. Writers be aware.

FORMAT

Because most soap operas are videotaped on sets, the likelihood is that they are three camera productions.

In terms of format there are two choices—a single column format or a double column format.

A single column is organized on the right two-thirds of the page. Description is capitalized, including stage directions. Camera descriptions are capitalized but distinct from scene description.

Dialogue is set off from the capitalized name of the speaker. The double-spaced dialogue is not capitalized. Description is single spaced. What follows is a sample of the two column format.

TITLE OF SHOW

Episode: _____

Writer: _____

First Draft.   Date Contact: name

                                           address

                                           phone

VIDEO	AUDIO
Fade in – on a small dinner party. The setting is elegant. The three people –Everett Street, his wife Elena and their guest Ivan Parker, are enjoying themselves.	
	IVAN: To our friendship.
	EVERETT: May it last a life time.
They drink and then throw their glasses into the fireplace.	
	The sound of glass shattering.
	ELENA: Or at least until tomorrow.
	IVAN: You are cynical about foreigners?
	ELENA: Not at all.
	EVERETT: She understands her husband.

```
                              ELENA: Better than he under-
                              stands his wife.

                              IVAN: I am an analyst. But
                              tonight I'd rather be your
                              friend.

                              ELENA: I'd like to be your
                              friend.
Everett is not pleased at the
turn of the conversation.
END OF SCENE.
```

Noteworthy about the format is the capitalization of single spaced description and the double spacing of non-capitalized dialogue.

This spacing results in the proportion of approximately two pages of script to about 1 minute of film time.

12

▼
▼
▼
▼
▼

Writing a Police/Detective/ Doctor/Lawyer Story

Every television series has as its underlying agenda to create a whole world into which the viewer chooses to enter and reenter. Viewers reenter because they like/ admire/love the characters and the world view of those characters. That world view is the philosophy, attitude, or point of view of the show.

Police/detective/doctor/lawyer stories choose to reorder their world through goals and attitudes of the main character. And always the struggle of that character is to better their world or to survive their world. Their struggle is a heroic struggle, a worthy struggle, a moral struggle. And this is the factor that brings audiences back week after week.

Lou Grant is the crusading newspaper editor who wants to improve his society. Dr. Kildare is the good doctor who must learn that intentions are not enough to overcome the realities of the natural world—people die, and some carry on; in other words, the good doctor can save life, but only sometimes.

The challenge for the writer of this type of series is to find a character and then to marry that character to the philosophy of the show. But critically important is for the writer to realize that in writing a particular series, you are creating a world and a way of seeing the world. Which is why the best series have a distinct sense of place and people and often a distinctive "world." Think of "Miami Vice" or "St. Else-where" or "Hill Street Blues." Each has a distinct sense of place; they are a world unto themselves.

THE IMPORTANCE OF THE MAIN CHARACTER

In series such as these, the critical pivotal role of the main character is central. The main character may be a policeman or a lawyer or a doctor; differing professions, but a similar moral position.

In the 1960s there were variations upon the young generic hero (like Kildare). The blind detective or the wheelchair-confined detective were temporarily popular. These variations have been replaced by the flawed personal life—the divorced captain in "Hill Street Blues," the materialistic lawyer in "L.A. Law"; but all of these variations don't mask the true nature of the main character.

In all cases the main character's mission in life is to make the world a better place. He finds flaws in the system and he tries to seek out the best solution in spite of the system.

In terms of goals, the character is definitely a hero. This means big challenges and big antagonists.

It also means a sense of indignation about the status quo. And a rather aggressive approach to problem solving. Both qualities make the main character attractive as a hero.

THE OTHER CHARACTERS

The world of the main character must be populated by men and women who fill out the sense of moral options. This ranges from the moralistic to the amoral to the immoral. This not only gives context for the actions of the hero; it also provides a patina of realism, for our world is, in fact, made up of such gradations.

Other characters cross age/sex/race/religion lines to provide a reflection closer to the world we live in. The best shows like "Hill Street Blues" give much time to develop these characters.

A few of these characters are worth highlighting. Often the older, more experienced "father figure" is one of those characters (recall Raymond Massey in "Dr. Kildare"). Another is the sidekick (Noah Berry in "The Rockford Files"). Another is the boss (Cybill Shepherd in "Moonlighting") and, of course, the love interest (Veronica Hammel in "Hill Street Blues").

Generally the continuing characters are variations on these "types." In "Charlie's Angels" the hero(es) are the angels—the three beautiful detectives with Charlie, the "father figure" never seen. The love interest may be male or female, wives or lovers, and sidekicks can have a cross-cultural character or a cross-class character. Each show seems to look for its own new and distinct variation.

A word about the antagonist. In most of these shows the antagonist is not a continuing character, but rather a person introduced each week. It may be a person with an incurable disease or a gangster who threatens the delicate urban equilibrium between law and anarchy.

This is the role of the "guest star" of each episode. What is critical is to what degree this character, his condition, and goals be opposed to that of the main character. And the greater the challenge this character poses, the more likely the struggle will affirm the heroic nature of the main character.

THE ROLE OF THE SETTING IN CREATING A HEROIC CHARACTER

A large urban newspaper, a small rural law practice, a police hierarchy working within an urban jungle, a police hierarchy at work in an urban paradise, each setting sets the parameters for the challenges to the main character.

Miami is a paradise that is corrupted by drugs. In this world of fast cars, beautiful women, where weapons and Georgio Armani coexist, the main characters have to adopt the coloration of their habitat. A Lou Grant main character wouldn't work in this setting. And so Sonny is superficially like the environment. It is only his intentions that make him different from his enemies, the corrupt criminals of Miami Vice. And the temptations of the setting are so great that he has to be all the more alert to his goals in order to function in this setting. Part of the show however requires Sonny to live by the values of the setting—hedonism, materialism abound. But they don't make him less of a hero. In fact he has to transcend these superficial elements and in doing so, he is a hero.

THE ROLE OF THE PROBLEM IN CREATING A HEROIC CHARACTER

Like situation comedies, each episode poses a particular problem for the main character. In the police/detective/doctor/lawyer story it is critical that this problem have a personal dimension for the main character.

What the writer should avoid is the episode where the problem is far removed from the main character. The case where the doctor proves he is a great surgeon is not quite good enough. We know he is a great, talented surgeon. The case is different when the patient is a wife or lover or parent or friend. Then what is at risk is the future of that personal relationship. What will the good doctor do in this more complex circumstance? In being human and meeting the challenges, we will once again see him as a true hero. This is why the episodic stories are so often personal stories where the main character has more than his career at risk.

Consequently, the problem posed every week should have a personal dimension for the main character. If it does, we, the audience, can become more involved with this person, the main character, who we long to see in heroic terms.

HEROES DON'T TALK LIKE ORDINARY PEOPLE

"Matlock" (Andy Griffith) has special insights into human behavior. Consequently, he wins cases. Magnum (Tom Selleck in "Magnum, P.I.") is low-key and self-effacing in his dialogue, the opposite of David Addison (Bruce Willis in "Moonlighting"), who is voluble and whose dialogue is an energetic clickety-clack of wit. And yet both are detectives in search of recourse for their clients.

The main point in each case is that the main character has distinctive dialogue, very different from all the other characters in the series.

The dialogue serves to set the main character off and helps us consider them in a different light. Without this distinction, the heroic stature would be more of a challenge for the writer.

Dialogue plays an important role in each case in preparing the audience to consider the main character a hero.

THE STORY

In the doctor series, the challenge is the never ending issues of medical illness, both from the vantage point of new cures and the limits of medical science. Each new case may be solved, but it is at best an interim solution. The result is that whatever the problem the main character solves in the course of an episode, the solution is a stop gap measure in the life vs. death struggle.

This means more cases, but it also suggests that some problems will be solved but others won't be. What is critical to the audience is that the struggle be a heroic struggle.

The story then should revolve around a medical case. In the police story, the problem will revolve around a particular crime. In the detective story, the problem will involve a particular investigation. And in the lawyer story, the problem will involve an accusation and consequent trial. In most series the lawyer is acting on behalf of the defendant. This positions the lawyer in a heroic position (whereas the crown prosecutor appears to have the less heroic authority and the power of government on his side.)

In all of these series solutions are part of the long term struggle for justice and well-being. Important is that the struggle is ongoing. One case, one episode, one victim on a long road, is another quality of all these types of series.

The problem makes up the story line but as with all of episodic series, there has to be more than one story ongoing. Generally, the second story, whether it is the major story or the secondary story, will have a more personalized dimension for the character. Whether it is a love story or a parent-child story, its base is emotional.

The major story and the minor story should have ample twists and turns to keep the viewer involved. And above all the task of both stories is to demonstrate the heroic struggle of the main character.

A point worth making again about story in these types of series is that, as often as possible, the stories tend to be strong personal interest stories.

THE IMPORTANCE OF DIALOGUE

Many stories have strong visual character or setting (Hawaii, Miami, New York) and interesting central characters ("Cagney and Lacey," "Remington Steele," "Columbo"): But in each case the dialogue is distinctive. In "Cagney and Lacey," the dialogue is passionate and realistic. In "Remington Steele" the dialogue is witty and tinged with seductiveness. In "Columbo" the dialogue is ironic and deliberate. Perhaps no show is as well known for its dialogue as "Moonlighting."

What is critical in each series is that the dialogue is engaging and energized. Like the situation comedy, dialogue is used to bring us closer to the thoughts and intentions of the characters. Because television is a medium of pace and involvement, the dialogue is a critical factor in hastening our relationship with characters. Consequently, the writer has to be sensitive to the importance of dialogue and skilled in its usage.

STRUCTURE

These one hour series tend to follow an Act I - Act II - Act III - Act IV - Epilogue structure.

In Act I the problem, the major story is introduced. In the police story this involves a crime. The perpetrator is introduced. Similarly in the medical show the illness is introduced.

In all cases the crime or illness are visualized in action. In the course of this action the real antagonist—a criminal or an illness is introduced.

Having brought the case and the main character into contact, the secondary, more personal story, is also introduced in Act I.

Where possible the secondary story complicates the major story (as is the case in the soap opera).

The first act ends in a crisis (the appropriate point to go to a commercial).

Act II and Act III are the acts where the plot becomes increasingly complicated. The main character becomes increasingly invested in the dramatic situation. This may take the form of a personal involvement with the victim or the accused.

Through Act II and Act III the issue of the life and death struggle must be highlighted. The victim has nothing less than his life in the balance. If the main character is personally involved with the victim or accused, the result is that his future is also at risk.

Throughout these two acts the power of the antagonist, whether it be the criminal or the prosecutor or the illness, has to be demonstrated in action. Only by this type of demonstration do we understand how much the main character must overcome.

Here the development of dramatic values—conflict, twists and turns, the nature of the antagonist—is at its strongest.

And it is in Act II and Act III that the nature of the series—its character-orientation, or its plot-orientation, its naturalism ("Hill Street Blues") or its non-naturalism ("Moonlighting"), becomes a critical story element to offset the emphasis on character or plot.

It is in Act II and III when we are between setup and resolution that strong dialogue and atmosphere become important to sustain our involvement with this particular episode.

At the end of Act III another crisis sets the story on the road toward resolution.

Act IV, the act where the resolution in both the major and the minor stories occur, is an act filled with activity. We rush to the resolution in Act IV. And it is in Act IV when the true test of the main character is put to the test. This is where the defense lawyer figures out who the real killer is; or where the capture of a criminal takes place through the application of investigative techniques; or when the operation on the incurable patient succeeds or fails.

Act IV is the test for the main character. In Act IV our confidence in that character has to be affirmed. Resolution comes from the effort, the act, on the part of the main character.

Finally, the episode ends with an epilogue where the main character no longer has to act in a super-human way. Indeed, the epilogue affirms his or her humanity. This brief reminder re-establishes our connection with the main character. And we are ready for his or her effort to enter a heroic struggle again next week.

THE SOAP OPERA EFFECT

Very often these weekly series have a very particular character and plotting. And even the naturalistic series—"Hill Street Blues" and "L.A. Law"—borrow a great deal from the soap opera.

Heightened emotions, polarized situations, the utilization of major life dilemmas, are all prevalent dimensions of these stories.

Whenever possible the scales of life and death are brought to bear. This requires a suspension of belief on our part. No one goes from the frying pan into the fire week after week, except in soap operas.

We accept this type of hyperdrama for a variety of reasons.

1. We are attracted to the main character.
2. We identify with the world view of the main character.
3. The setting for the drama is appealing.
4. We want to view the struggles of everyday life in heroic terms; and the main character is a hero.
5. We are assured that these practitioners that affect our lives in the realm of law, order, and good health, have as their goals the betterment of society.

Just as we wish to be the richest, sexiest person anywhere, these continuing characters offer up the moral, rather than materialistic fantasy. They are the moral center in their world. And they offer us the opportunity to transcend the position of victim and to identify with "the knights of our society".

LEAVE THEM FEELING GOOD

In this sense it is critical to leave the audience satisfied. They have to feel that the main character has struggled and most of the time overcome the challenge.

It is very important in this moral struggle that the main character be viewed as making the effort week after week. If we believe in the character, we will feel good for that struggle.

In this sense, the hero in the police/detective/doctor/lawyer series plays the same role as the western hero used to play prior to the advent of television.

But now in a modern, often urban setting, we haven't lost the idealistic fantasy that there are individuals who struggle with the forces of modernity and who win. This is the primary importance of these series, and the reason why the success of these characters is important to us. It affirms our sense of a world we would like to live in.

The writer has to understand these issues and to view the struggle of the main character in a heroic fashion. It isn't enough to view writing episodic television as plot development. It is critical for the writer to realize the heroic dimension of these stories and to develop the script to allow this dimension of episodic television to be prominent.

Format

THE CASE OF NO REMORSE

An episode of _____.
            by _____.

for: production company address.

First Draft   contact: name
                                       address
                                       phone

A well-decorated apartment. A man is fixing himself a
drink. He appears alone but expecting someone.

In the dining room, two place settings suggest he will be
entertaining.

He goes into the kitchen and comes out and places two
steaming servings at each place setting. He sits down and
begins to eat.

There is a knock at the door.

He seems pleased.

He opens to door. We don't see who enters. But the person
follows him in.

                        MAN
    I'll make you a drink.

He approaches the bar. He mixes the drink. He turns to offer
the drink. A shot is fired and he falls, surprised.

CUT TO: INT. INVESTIGATOR'S OFFICE - DAY

MAT LONDON is drinking coffee. His assistant is telling him
about his appointments for the day.

                    ASSISTANT
    A few more weeks of this and you'll need to get a real job.

                        MAT
    Where are all the widows when I need them?

There is a knock at the door.

                    ASSISTANT
    Right on cue.

The Assistant goes to the door. A beautiful woman dressed in
black enters. The Assistant looks her over.

                              WOMAN
      Is Mr. London here?

                            ASSISTANT
      Every business hour.

                              WOMAN
      I have business for him.

                            ASSISTANT
      I'm sure he'll see you.

A few seconds later the Assistant shows her into the inner office. Mat London offers her his hand.

                              WOMAN
      I'm Caroline Dale.

                               MAT
      Please sit down.

                              WOMAN
      You have to help me. Money is no object.

                               MAT
      What can I do for you?

                              WOMAN
      My husband has been killed.

                               MAT
      What have the police found?

                              WOMAN
      You don't understand. I killed my husband!

Mat is more than perplexed.
END OF SCENE.

That's the end of our discussion of writing a police/detective/doctor/lawyer story. Now it's time for you to begin the next phase—the writing.

In this book I've tried to help you with the form and the formats of various genres of broadcast writing. Whether it's a police story or a situation comedy or a radio documentary you undertake, you should try to enjoy it.

Good luck and enjoy the writing!